CW00738709

THE FOOTBALL GODS ARE REAL: VOLUME 1

.

The FOOTBALL GODS *are* REAL

Vol. 1: THE RELIGION *of* FOOTBALL

JONATHAN A. FINK

author of *The Baseball Gods Are Real*

The Religion of Football
by Jonathan A. Fink
Copyright 2023

Polo Grounds Publishing LLC

Credit and thank you to Meg Reid for book cover design and book layout.

Credit and thank you to Meg Schader for editing.

Credit and thank you to Abi Laksono for the Polo Grounds Publishing logo.

Credit and thank you to Kim Watson for biography photo.

This book is dedicated to Tate Myre, The Hero

TABLE OF CONTENTS

PREFACE

"After all, is football a game or a religion?"
—Howard Cosell

IN 2018, I PUBLISHED MY FIRST BOOK: *THE Baseball Gods are Real: A True Story About Baseball and Spirituality.* The book was autobiographical and chronicled the first forty-two years of my life. I discussed my love of baseball and many of the important events in my life, including a midlife crisis at the age of thirty-eight which inspired me to explore a spiritual path. A few chapters in the book revealed how I transformed myself through the practice of yoga and meditation. At about the same time, I was introduced to one of the mysterious forces in the universe, the work of the Baseball Gods.

In my second book, *The Baseball Gods are Real–Volume 2: The Road to the Show,* I continued on my spiritual journey and chronicled the next chapters of my life. After thirteen years as a financial advisor with Morgan Stanley, I started my own investment firm, Satya Investment Management.

Thereafter, I had a chance encounter with professional baseball player Jon Perrin, who was working at a restaurant at that time, an off-season job. A blossoming friendship led to his apprenticeship with me, which eventually led him to join my firm as a professionally licensed investment advisor. This second book also chronicled Perrin's own journey through baseball's minor league system, from his early days climbing the ranks in the Milwaukee Brewers organization to his eventual trade to the Kansas City Royals.

In the third book in the series, *The Baseball Gods are Real–Volume 3: The Religion of Baseball*, I paid homage to the Baseball Gods and set out to praise all things related to baseball and spirituality. The book commemorated baseball miracles, celebrated baseball's cathedrals, applauded baseball's saints, and called out its sinners. The book also acknowledged the baseball fanatics, whom I affectionally referred to as the zealots, and magnified many of the rituals and superstitions that help make baseball the wonderful, mysterious, enjoyable game it is. Finally, *Baseball Gods Vol. 3* explored baseball karma, examined freak injuries, and even investigated the paranormal world of baseball, including baseball tales of ghosts and, believe it or not, UFOs. After publishing *The Baseball Gods are Real* books, it occurred to me that I could also write books about the Basketball Gods, the Hockey Gods, and even — The Football Gods.

On December 10, 2018, the last night of Chanukah, my father-in-law, Sam Devinki, called and invited me to the upcoming Kansas City Chiefs game on December 13th, a rare Thursday night home game. The Kansas City Chiefs were hosting their rivals the San Diego Chargers and Sam told me that Rabbi Moshe Grussgott, who had just moved to Kansas City from Philadelphia, would be joining us. When I found out that Rabbi Grussgott loved the game of baseball and was a Philadelphia Phillies fan, we had much to discuss on the way to the game.

Shortly after we sat in our seats and started watching the game, we had our first "Football Gods" moment. The stadium announcer recognized and honored a member of the United States military, a tradition at every home Chiefs game. I don't remember the soldier's first name, nor his army rank or even his job in the military, but I will never forget the soldier's last name. It was — Maccabee.

Now for those of you not familiar, the Jewish holiday of Chanukah is based on the story about "Judah and The Maccabees." The Maccabees were the priestly family of Jews who organized a successful rebellion against the Syrian Empire. Judah Maccabee led the revolt against the Syrian army. The Jewish holiday of Chanukah, also spelled Hanukkah, earned the nicknamed "the festival of lights" because of a miracle. As the story goes, the miracle occurred after the liberation of the city of Jerusalem.

After defeating the Syrians on the battlefield, the Maccabees returned to Jerusalem and to the Temple. They wanted to rededicate the Temple and perform religious rituals. One of the rituals was the lighting of the Menorah, a large branched candlestick, but the Menorah could only be lit with pure olive oil and the Maccabees could only retrieve enough oil for the lamp to light for one day. However, a miracle occurred and the Menorah stayed lit and shined

JONATHAN FINK

bright for eight days. This is why the holiday of Chanukah is celebrated for eight days and nights.

There I was, sitting next to our synagogue's new rabbi, just three days after the Chanukah holiday and the army veteran being honored was an officer with the last name Maccabee. I turned to Rabbi Grussgott and said, "What are the odds that Chanukah just ended, we are at the Chiefs game with our new rabbi, and the soldier being honored has the last name Maccabee?" I directed my father-in-law, Sam, to watch the big screen just as the cameraman was focusing on the soldier's uniform and clear as day, you could see the badge with the last name on it. I looked at Rabbi Grussgott again in amazement and said with excitement, "The Football Gods are real!"

My father-in-law is notorious for always wanting to leave Arrowhead Stadium with five minutes left on the fourth quarter clock to beat the traffic. To be fair, exiting a parking lot with 80,000 fans can be cumbersome and frustrating at times. When the Chiefs are winning or losing big, I never complain. However, whenever Sam wants to leave early during a very close game, I don't like it. It always feels disrespectful to the Football Gods. Well, on this night, the Kansas City Chiefs were up 14–7 at halftime. At the end of the third quarter, the Chiefs were beating the Chargers 21–14. At the time, the Chiefs were in first place in their division with an impressive 11–2 record. As the fourth quarter reached the five-minute mark, the Chiefs were winning by the score of 28–14. Sam turned to me and the rabbi and said, "C'mon, let's go." I rebutted, "Sam, it's the rabbi's first game at Arrowhead. I know the Chiefs are winning, but the Chargers have the ball and they are marching down the field!" Sam was not having it and he nodded his head no. I turned to Rabbi Grussgott and said, "The Football Gods will not be pleased."

We listened to the game on the radio as we drove home. Chargers quarterback Philip Rivers threw a deep ball into the end zone trailing 28–14 and the Chiefs were called for pass interference by the referee. On the next play, the Chargers ran it in for a touchdown. I said, "This is not good. We have upset the Football Gods. It's bad luck to leave at the end of a very close game!" With three minutes remaining on the clock, the Chargers forced a third down and 13 and managed to sack Chiefs quarterback Patrick Mahomes, forcing Kansas City to punt. The Chargers moved the ball forward to the Chiefs' 40-yard line as Sam pulled into my driveway to drop me off. I stayed in the car with Sam and Rabbi Grussgott to listen to the end of the game. On the next play, Rivers completed a pass to earn a first down. The Chargers had the ball on the Chiefs' 10-yard line at third and goal. Rivers tried to hit a wide receiver in the end zone, but the Chiefs got called for another pass interference penalty. The Chargers now had first and goal, from the one-yard line, with four seconds left in the game. Touchdown Chargers! Philip Rivers connected with wide receiver Mike Williams in the end zone. The Chargers decide to forego kicking the extra point and go for the two-point conversion. Philips found Williams in the end zone again. The two-point conversion was successful! Game over. It was the Chargers' first lead of the night. Final score: Chargers 29, Chiefs 28. Stunned, but not entirely surprised, I said, "The Football Gods are real." I opened the car door, thanked Sam for the game invite, told Rabbi Grussgott it was great to meet him, and said goodnight as I closed the car door.

Walking away from the car towards my house, I thought to myself that one day, down the road, I am going to write a book about the Football Gods. That night, I created a file in my office called "The Football Gods are Real" and began collecting articles related to football and spirituality. Three years went by and my stack of research had become substantial. But on December 4th, 2021, the sixth night of Chanukah, I knew it was time to write this book because that was the night that I learned about — The Story of Tate Myre.

INTRODUCTION

"Baseball is what we were. Football is what we have become."
—Mary McGrory

IN THIS BOOK, *THE FOOTBALL GODS ARE REAL—VOL. 1: The Religion of Football*, I pay homage to the Football Gods and set out to praise all things related to football and spirituality. The book focuses on the religiosity of football, celebrates football's cathedrals, applauds football's saints, and calls out its sinners. The book also acknowledges the football fanatics, whom I affectionally refer to as the zealots, and magnifies many of the traditions, rivalries, rituals, and superstitions that help make football the wonderful, mysterious, enjoyable game it is. This book explores football karma and the dark side of football, and searches for the fingerprints of the Football Gods from beginning to end. It also celebrates serendipitous moments and even investigates the paranormal world of football, including tales of curses, ghosts, and — believe it or not — UFOs. Breaking tackles like a power running back and heading towards the end zone, this book revisits the American dream and looks ahead to the golden age of football yet to come.

CHAPTER ONE

The Story of Tate Myre

"God works in mysterious ways."
—Aiden Hutchinson

ON NOVEMBER 27, 2021, OXFORD HIGH SCHOOL football player Tate Myre was on a recruiting trip to visit the University of Toledo. The 16-year-old junior, who played linebacker and running back for the Oxford Wildcats, watched with excitement as the Toledo Rockets defeated the Akron Zips 49–14. The next day, Myre made a post on the social media platform Twitter. Showing his gratitude and character, he wrote, "Had a great time at the Toledo game yesterday. Thank you Coach Ricky Ciccone and Toledo Football for the invite!" Driving home from Toledo, Ohio, to his small town in the suburbs of Detroit, Michigan, Myre must have felt like he was living in a blissful dream. Not too many high school football players get recruited to play college football at the Division 1 level. However, just two days after returning from his recruiting trip, tragedy struck Oxford, Michigan, and Tate Myre's joyful dream life quickly turned into a horrific nightmare.

On Tuesday, November 30, 2021, in between classes at Oxford High School, Tate Myre was walking amongst the swarm of high school students scampering to get to their next class. The hallways were packed with hundreds of students, when a crazed, deranged, and vengeful 15-year-old sophomore emerged from the boy's bathroom with a semiautomatic handgun and began shooting. Chaos ensued. According to the students, a voice over the intercom alerted them to an active shooter and the teachers began locking and barricading doors and covering windows as they tried to convince the students that this was not a drill. The police were called in and would arrive in the next few minutes.

During the violent commotion, as students were running scared and terrified, Tate Myre rushed the shooter in an attempt to disarm him and give his classmates time to get away. He suffered multiple gunshot wounds in the process and died on the way to the hospital. Four students were killed and several people, including a teacher, were badly wounded. No doubt that Myre saved lives that day as he sacrificed his own.

Members of the Oxford community set up an online petition hoping to honor and remember Tate Myre. The petition's goal was to rename Oxford's football stadium after Myre. The petition read, "Tate is not just a hero to his fellow students at Oxford high school but a legend. His act of bravery should be remembered forever and passed down through generations." The following Saturday, Myre's courage and bravery was honored by the University of Michigan football team.

The Michigan Wolverines, despite being recognized as

one of the best college football programs in the country, had not won a Big Ten Conference football championship in 17 years. Hard to believe. Perhaps the team had been cursed for all those years. Well, in the religion of football, acts of good karma get the attention of the Football Gods and when enough good karma is built up, good things will certainly follow, and even long-held curses can be broken. Michigan Wolverines defensive end senior Aidan Hutchinson and his teammates and coaches were about to find out. According to Michigan's head coach Jim Harbaugh, "Aidan came to me and said he wanted to dedicate this game to Tate Myre." Coach Harbaugh replied, "Yes, let's do that." Coach Harbaugh took the idea to Warde Manuel, Michigan's athletic director, and he handled the rest.

When the Michigan Wolverines took the field in the Big Ten Championship game on December 4, 2021, the Myre family joined the players on the field for the coin toss. Tate's family members were honorary team captains for the game. Standing at the coin flip in front of the referees, the Iowa Hawkeyes football team and tens of thousands of fans, they wore shirts that read "Oxford Strong." Myre's family members were not the only ones wearing special shirts. The Michigan Wolverines wore a patch on their jerseys with the initials "TM." The patch had Tate Myre's football jersey number 42 under the TM. There were also four hearts to honor Tate and his classmates who tragically died that day — Hana St. Juliana, Madisyn Baldwin, and Justin Shilling.

With the holy spirit flowing through everyone on their team, the Michigan Wolverines played their hearts out and yes indeed, defeated the Iowa Hawkeyes to win their first Big Ten football championship since 2004. When the Michigan players noticed the scoreboard, they had to pause to appreciate the final score: 42–3. Michigan had scored 42 points! Aidan Hutchinson and his teammates looked at the scoreboard in awe. After the game, Hutchinson told reporters, "God works in mysterious ways." Offensive lineman Andrew Vastardis said, "It's up to God, man. To score 42 points? It gave me chills when I noticed that."

In the post-game press conference, Michigan head coach Jim Harbaugh, without knowing it perhaps, was talking directly to the Football Gods and making his case for why Tate Myre deserves sainthood. Referring to Myre, Harbaugh said, "Tate was a warrior. Football player, wrestler, best athlete in school. The best athlete in school could have easily made it out, been the first one out, but while people were running away from fire, he was running into it. He was a hero." Coach Harbaugh, clearly well versed in the religion of football, referred to the importance of prayer when he told reporters, "It's a community that needs all of our prayer. We wanted to offer that up. We wanted to offer our prayers to a community that desperately needs it." The next day in the National Football League would prove to be equally as remarkable and poignant.

The Detroit Lions hosted the Minnesota Vikings on December 5, 2021. During warmups, many of the Lions players and coaches were wearing "Oxford Strong" T-shirts. Even Vikings Quarterback Kirk Cousins wore an "Oxford Wildcats" T-shirt during warmups and both teams wore an "O" decal on their helmets. When the game was about to begin and the players ran on to the field, Michigan football fans watching live at Ford Field along with those watching in sports bars and in their homes all across the state must have felt the emotional surge when Detroit Lions safety, Jalen Elliot emerged from the stadium tunnel wearing a No. 42 customized jersey with "Myre" on the back as fans all around the stadium held signs that read "Oxford Strong."

The Detroit Lions had been the worst team in the league. They were the only team to be winless during the 2021 season. They had not won a home game in front of their fans in a year. And yet, the Football Gods were up to the task. As time expired, Lions quarterback Jared Goff found Amon-Ra St. Brown open in the end zone. Goff threw St. Brown an 11-yard pass for the game-winning touchdown. The final score was 29–27. The fans, the coaches, and the players celebrated like crazy! In the locker room after the game, Lions head coach Dan Campbell was awarded the game ball, and minutes later, he met the media for his post-game press conference.

When first-year head coach Dan Campbell began his press conference comments, the first thing he did was dedicate the game ball to the Oxford community. He then read the names of the ten students and one teacher injured and the four students killed. He said, "I want us to not forget these names....For all those — they'll never be forgotten, they're in our hearts and our prayers, and all the families — not to mention all those that were affected by all of this. The classmates, the brothers and sisters, the cousins, the teachers, everybody." Hana St. Juliana, Madisyn Baldwin, Justin Shilling, and Tate Myre, may your souls rest in peace.

CHAPTER TWO

The Faithful

"God blessed me to play football."
—Terrell Owens

MOST RELIGIOUS DEVOTEES WORSHIP A HIGHER POWER. This higher power is said to be God, believed to be a supreme being that governs and controls the ways of the world. The concept of God, as described by theologians, commonly includes the attributes of an all-knowing, all-powerful, invisible, and all-present deity. While the Abrahamic religions are monotheistic, thus believing in just one God, in the religion of football, players, coaches, sports reporters, and fans worship a collection of supreme deities known as — The Football Gods.

Sometimes the Football Gods are portrayed as kind, loving, and gentle overlords. When good things happen to our favorite team or player, the Football Gods are praised for their acts of generosity and benevolence. Other times, the Football Gods are portrayed as angry and vengeful. When bad things happen to our favorite team or player, the Football Gods are held responsible, having forsaken us or even cursed us.

One thing is for certain, five of our planet's major religions — Christianity, Islam, Hinduism, Buddhism and Judaism — all reference angels in their religious scriptures and portray angels to be celestial or atmospheric spirits who intervene in human affairs on this earthly plane. Whether it's the work of heavenly angels or by the hands of God, football players, coaches, sportswriters and fans who have learned about or experienced the mysterious ways of the Football Gods know that it's a good idea to stay in their good graces.

On a more serious note, "The Football Gods" is just a nickname for God, the father of Jesus Christ. The same God who is worshipped in the Torah and the Bible by the Israelites, and the same God worshipped by more than a billion Muslims around the world. While casual football fans and witty sports reporters may be lighthearted when referencing the Football Gods, faith in God is not a joking matter. In fact, many football players and coaches at the high school, college, and professional level take their faith in a higher power very seriously.

By definition, faith is confidence or trust in a person, thing, or concept. In the context of religion, faith is defined as "belief in God" or in the religious scriptures and teachings of a religion. Faith in Buddhism refers to a serene commitment to the practice of the Buddha's teachings and trust in enlightened or highly developed individuals well on their way to reaching enlightenment. In Islam, a believer's faith in the metaphysical aspects of Islam is called Iman.

According to the Quran, Iman must be accompanied by righteous deeds and the two together are necessary for entry into the final home of the righteous, also referred to as Paradise. Followers of Christianity agree that the Christian faith is aligned with the ideals and the examples of the life of Jesus Christ. In Hinduism faith has a wider meaning. Faith in the creator God is not central to many schools of Hinduism. However, faith in the Self and its eternal existence is important.

The deep faith football coaches and players have in a higher power is self-evident. Many high school, college, and professional teams pray together before games. Frequently after games, football players from both teams can be seen praying together. Lots of football players look to the sky and hold a finger up in their air to give thanks to their creator when they score a touchdown. When a player gets badly injured during a game, football players from both teams kneel down on the field and pray for him.

There is a long tradition of NFL football coaches and players mixing sports and religion. In 2017, the Philadelphia Eagles were big-time underdogs on their road to the Super Bowl. It turns out that quarterbacks Carson Wentz and Nick Foles were outspoken about their faith. The team's faith in a higher power was a common thread that bonded the team. The success of the team led to a book called *Birds of Pray* which cited faith as a key to the team's success.

In recent times, National Football League head coaches such as Tom Landry, Joe Gibbs, Dan Reeves and Tony Dungy have become well known for incorporating faith into their coaching style and infusing religious values into the team's locker room. Now at the college level, some renowned coaches have made headlines for their devotion to their faith and how they incorporate their belief in a higher power into their football programs.

At Ole Miss, former head coach Hugh Freeze met with his coaches and players every Sunday for church services and Bible study. Sometimes the players led the service and Coach Freeze would tweet about it. Dan Mullen, the former head coach of Mississippi State's football program, is also known to tweet about his faith. University of Colorado head coach Deon Sanders makes Instagram posts about his faith in God frequently. There is another well-known college football coach that is a man of faith — Dabo Swinney, head coach at Clemson University.

It is well documented how much Dabo Swinney is devoted to his Christian faith. The charismatic coach is well known for attracting football players that are devoted faithful followers of Christianity and faith transcends the football program. The team even has their own chaplain. He leads a Bible study for coaches twice a week. The night before each game, nearly every player attends a voluntary chapel service. The team made headlines in 2013 when they held a baptism for one of their players during football practice.

Coach Swinney halted all the player drills and requested that the players and coaches gather around him near the 50-yard line. He told everyone that wide receiver DeAndre Hopkins had decided to turn his life over to Jesus Christ. Hopkins, still fully dressed in his football uniform, stepped into a livestock trough that was filled with water. Right then and there, a dozen players and coaches looked on as Hopkins was baptized.

There is one college football program that may be more faithful than even Clemson University, and that is the University of Notre Dame. On campus, the private Catholic university in South Bend, Indiana, has a giant mural depicting Jesus Christ on the side of the campus library building. The "Word of Life" mural can be seen directly from within Notre Dame Stadium. The mural has a nickname — Touchdown Jesus.

Many sports fanatics literally pray for their favorite team to win football games. However, it is important to point out that most faithful coaches, players, and chaplains concur that God does not care who wins any particular game. In fact, most religious coaches and players believe that praying for victory is inappropriate. If you asked most football chaplains, they would tell you that before a game, coaches and players should pray to God to help them do their best and avoid injury. That old saying is true when it comes to the faithful, it doesn't matter if you win or lose, it comes down to character and integrity and how you play the game.

CHAPTER THREE

The Religiosity of Football

"Five days shalt thou labour, as the Bible says. The seventh day is
the Lord thy God's. The sixth day is for football."
—Anthony Burgess

THERE ARE A NUMBER OF INTERESTING SIMILARITIES
between football and organized religion. Football stadiums
are beautiful and individually unique as are churches, synagogues, temples, and mosques. The game of football is filled
with ceremony, tradition, ritual, numerology, and superstition just like many religions in the world. Many who closely
follow the game of football worship the sport, make sacri-
fices, pray for their team, and suffer when their team loses.
These emotions are also common in religion. Football and
organized religion both offer a sense of community, hope,
faith, and their followers believe in miracles.

Today, the game of football is the most popular sport

in the United States. In fact, more than 40 percent of Americans identify either professional or college football as their favorite sport. Less than 10 percent of Americans today consider baseball their favorite sport. To better appreciate how Americans became so passionate about the game of football, a look back at the prehistory of the game would be beneficial.

While today football is the most popular sport amongst the masses, it did not start out that way. In fact, the game of football emerged in the United States as a college sport played exclusively by the Ivy League universities. In the 1800s, Walter Camp invented the game of football after extracting out the essence of the game of rugby. The first football players in America were not blue-collar sons of miners from the mountains of West Virginia, but rather the sons of investment bankers and industrialists at universities such as Harvard, Yale, and Princeton.

Back in the day, college football players did not get scholarships to play like they do today. Playing football for Dartmouth as they faced off against their rivals at Cornell was motivation enough. The players played for pride and loyalty to their school. As students began to attend the Ivy League football games and root for their classmates, they also felt that sense of loyalty and school pride as their college played football against a rival school.

By the early 1900s, the popularity of football proliferated and midwestern farm boys and inner-city immigrants got to watch and play the game for the first time. For most Americans, watching their first football game was love at first sight. By end of the roaring 1920s, most colleges had their own football teams. Saturday and college football games during the autumn season had become sacred days for devoted college students and alumni. As the National Football League became as popular as college football, Sundays also became a sacred day for football fans. Perhaps not a coincidence, but as the National Football League became an American obsession in the 1950s and more fans started attending professional football games on Sunday, there was a decline in church attendance across the county that continues to this day.

An argument could be made that football is the new religion in the United States of America. Football has its own institutionalized system of attitudes, beliefs, and practices. There is conformity and devotion. Fans get dressed up special on game day, wearing their best team swag. Whether football fans are attending the games at the stadium or watching at home or in a sports bar, millions of Americans are choosing to do the same ritual every weekend for at least six months out of the year. The religion of football even has its own holiday that is equivalent to Easter or Christmas — The Super Bowl.

CHAPTER FOUR

The Cathedrals

"The supporters swayed forwards and backwards like waves
crashing on the shore."
—Jim Lowe

SINGER-SONGWRITER JIMMY BUFFETT IS KNOWN FOR saying that America does not have big beautiful gothic cathedrals like they do in Europe, but the United States has majestic baseball stadiums. Jimmy Buffett was onto something with that statement. Ballparks are the cathedrals in the religion of baseball, and in the religion of football, the stadium serves the same purpose. From the local high school in Bellevue, Nebraska, to Notre Dame Stadium in South Bend, Indiana, to the newly built Allegiant Stadium, the 1.8 million-square-foot world-class new home of the NFL's Las Vegas Raiders, America's football stadiums are indeed sacred ground.

LaVell Edwards Stadium, home to the BYU Cougars in Provo, Utah, is a football cathedral. Not only is the stadium located at a high altitude, literally close to the heavens, but the stadium sits right next to Y Mountain, which provides a stunning view. The home of the Boise State Broncos, Albertsons Stadium, with its one-of-a-kind blue turf, is certainly worthy of cathedral consideration. Folsom Field, the home of the Colorado Buffaloes, is another high-altitude stadium surrounded by beautiful mountains worthy of cathedral status. Some college football stadiums are worthy of cathedral status just because of their capacity to seat so many football fans in one place.

Kyle Field, the home of Texas A&M's football program in College Station, Texas, seats just over 100,000. Neyland Stadium, home to the Tennessee Volunteers, holds 102,000. Ohio Stadium in Columbus, Ohio, home to the Ohio State Buckeyes can fit 104,944. Michigan Stadium, home to the Michigan Wolverines seats 107,661. While some football stadiums are known for their size, other football stadiums are known for their nicknames.

The stadium where the University of Florida Gators play their home games is known as "The Swamp." The home of the Penn State Nittany Lions is known as "Happy Valley." Two university stadiums actually have the same nickname — the stadiums at Louisiana State University and Clemson University are both called "Death Valley." Ohio Stadium in Columbus, Ohio, is known as "The Horseshoe" and Michigan Stadium, in Ann Arbor, Michigan, is called "The Big House."

All of these college football cathedrals have their own

charm and each stadium around the United States has its own unique atmosphere, surrounding backdrop, and scenery. While college football stadiums such as Memorial Stadium in Lincoln, Nebraska, and Bryant-Denny Stadium in Tuscaloosa, Alabama, are each unique and special in their own way, there is nothing more unique and special than the college football stadiums scattered around the country dedicated just to what are known as "bowl games."

The term "bowl" became popular after the construction of Rose Bowl Stadium, site of the first postseason college football game. Rose Bowl Stadium, in Los Angeles, California, got its name and bowl-shaped design from the Yale Bowl, the home stadium of Yale University's football team in New Haven, Connecticut. The term has since become almost synonymous with any major football event. When two rival college teams play their annual game, it is called a bowl game like the Iron Bowl between Auburn and Alabama or the Egg Bowl between Mississippi State and Ole Miss. Even in the National Football League, the championship game is called the Super Bowl and the end of season All-Star game is called the Pro Bowl. While the sponsors and sometimes the stadiums can change from year to year, there are select few college bowl games and respective stadiums that have stood the test of time.

The Liberty Bowl is an annual American college football bowl game played in late December or early January since 1959. For its first five years, it was played in Philadelphia. Since 1965, the game has been held at Liberty Bowl Memorial Stadium in Memphis, Tennessee. The Cotton Bowl, located in Dallas, Texas, opened in 1930 as Fair

Park Stadium and hosted the State Fair of Texas. Starting in 1937, the 92,100-seat stadium hosted the first of 73 consecutive Cotton Bowl games. The Cotton Bowl today is now played at AT&T Stadium in Arlington, Texas, but Cotton Bowl Stadium still hosts the annual college football game between the Oklahoma Sooners and the Texas Longhorns. Also in Texas is the Sun Bowl. Since 1935, the Sun Bowl in El Paso, Texas, has hosted the annual college bowl game now known as the "Tony the Tiger Sun Bowl" named after the mascot of the Frosted Flakes cereal. The Sugar Bowl is an annual American college football bowl game played in New Orleans, Louisiana. Played annually since January 1, 1935, the Sugar Bowl was originally played at Tulane Stadium before moving to the Superdome in 1975.

As a member of the Bowl Championship Series, the Sugar Bowl hosted the BCS National Championship Game twice, in 2000 and 2004, as the national championship rotated between the bowls themselves until 2006 when the national championship game became a standalone event. Since the 2014 season, the Sugar Bowl has been in the rotation of bowls, commonly referred to as the New Year's Six, that host College Football Playoff (CFP) semifinal games once every three years.

From 1938 to 1996, the Orange Bowl was played annually at Miami Orange Bowl Stadium. Along with the Sun Bowl and the Sugar Bowl, the Orange Bowl is the one of the oldest bowls in the country. The Orange Bowl was located in the Little Havana neighborhood west of downtown Miami and it was considered a landmark. The stadium also was the home of the University of Miami Hurricanes and for more than twenty years, NFL's Miami Dolphins. Today, the Orange Bowl is played at Hard Rock Stadium in Miami Gardens, Florida. Now on to the "The Granddaddy of Them All," that of course is the nickname for — The Rose Bowl.

The Rose Bowl was first played in 1902 and is the oldest bowl game in the religion of football. The first game played at the Rose Bowl was known as the "Tournament East-West Football Game." The Rose Bowl is well known for its historic annual "Rose Parade" that precedes the big game. The stadium has been the home of the UCLA Bruins since 1982. There is actually another football cathedral in California that maybe even more grandiose than the Rose Bowl — The Los Angeles Coliseum.

The Los Angeles Memorial Coliseum, which seats 77,500, was built for civic pride in 1921 and serves as a living memorial to all who served in the U.S. Armed Forces during World War I. The stadium has been the home of the University of Southern California Trojans since 1923. The Los Angeles Coliseum has also hosted two Summer Olympics. The stadium is unmistakable with its pair of life-sized bronze statues of male and female athletes atop a 20,000-pound frame which forms the Olympic Gateway built before the Olympic Games in 1984.

Now, in the big spending, billion-dollar business of professional football, teams are constantly tearing down their football stadiums to build bigger and even better newer stadiums. However, a few relic stadiums have remained. In Chicago, Soldier Field still stands after its construction way back in 1924. Then there is legendary Lambeau Field in Green Bay, Wisconsin, which has been standing proud since 1957. In Kansas City, there is the glorious Arrowhead Stadium, which was built in 1972. New Era Field, formerly known as Ralph Wilson Stadium, in Buffalo, New York, deserves a shout-out, as it was built in 1973. Lastly, built in 1971, the New Orleans Superdome, home for many years to the Tulane Green Wave college football program and still today the home of NFL's New Orleans Saints. The Superdome has been hosts to many college football championship games and several NFL Super Bowls.

Every stadium mentioned in this chapter is a cathedral in the religion of football. While their physical characteristics, locations, and seating capacities are all different, inside these sacred buildings, the fans all share very similar experiences. Football stadiums are places of worship just like our country's churches, synagogues, and mosques. Devoted football fans come together and form a community of like-minded individuals. The fans sing songs in harmony together like a church choir. Together they glorify their players and team achievements on the field and feel sadness and remorse together when their favorite players disappoint them. The energy inside high school, college, and pro football stadiums is electric and the passion of the fans is contagious. Together, supporters of the same team perform rituals like chanting, clapping, and booing together, and the potential is at each game for miracle moments and spiritual experiences to take place.

While the football cathedrals are of course integral to the religion of football, the gameday experience lasts for longer than the three-hour football game held inside the stadium.

In fact, for many football fanatics, the gameday experience begins several hours before the game actually starts. Dedicated sports enthusiasts gather in stadium parking lots all across the country for hours before every football game to congregate. These die-hard football devotees enjoy food, drinks, listen to music, and play games. This pregame football experience is called — The Tailgate Party.

CHAPTER FIVE

The Tailgate Party

"Roses are red, mud is brown, round here we party with the
radio up and tailgate down."
—Earl Dibbles, Jr.

BY DEFINITION, A TAILGATE IS A BOARD OR GATE AT
the end of a vehicle, usually a truck, that can be removed
or let down, typically for loading things. However, since
the pregame party before each and every football game is
held in a football stadium parking lot, its nickname came
to be — The Tailgate Party. And in the religion of football,
the tailgate party has become an essential part of the game
day experience.

The activity of tailgating slowly grew in popularity
over the decades. Dedicated football fans began to bring
grills, coolers, and lawn chairs to the football stadium
and take over the empty parking lot spaces around their
cars and trucks. The tailgate of the truck became the hub
of friendly conversation, beer drinking, and hanging out.

Truly dedicated football fanatics took tailgating further still, bringing costumes, tents, flags, and logo-covered gear to their parties. Soon enough, "tailgating" became a movement.

Tailgate parties revolve around grilling food and consuming alcoholic beverages and soft drinks. It is customary for each guest to bring something to contribute to the party. It could be a six-pack of beer, a package of veggie burgers, or a tray of cookies. Everyone shares together and one group's tailgate party often will overlap with the tailgate group a few parking spots over. The most common eats at a football tailgate party include bratwurst, hamburgers, hot dogs, baked beans, barbeque ribs, coleslaw, potato salad, and lots of decadent deserts. In between the drinking and eating, tailgaters frequently play games in the parking lot.

The most popular tailgate games are lawn games such as horseshoes. In Kansas City, the most popular tailgate game is cornhole. Cornhole, also known as sack toss or bean bag toss, is a lawn game that can be played on grass or pavement. Players take turns throwing 16-ounce bags of corn kernels at a raised platform with a hole in the far end. A bag in the hole scores three points, while one on the board scores one point. Play continues until a team or player reaches or exceeds the score of 21.

The tailgate party today is an American institution. But no matter the location of the get-together, the tailgate event is an essential part of the gameday experience. Without question, in the religion of football, the tailgate party is the most commonly held tradition.

CHAPTER SIX

The Traditions

"You can learn more character on the two-yard line than
anywhere else in life."
—Paul Dietzel

A TRADITION IS A BELIEF OR BEHAVIOR PASSED DOWN
within a group or society with symbolic meaning or special
significance with origins in the past. Without question,
football is a game of pageantry and tradition. High school,
college, and professional football fans love their fight songs,
student sections, mascots, and marching bands. Players long
to earn a helmet sticker after a great game and hope after
their career is over to have their uniform number retired.
The traditions help make football such a great game.

Many traditions revolve around game day activities
inside the football stadium. At Lane Stadium, the home
of Virginia Tech University, the Hokies players enter the
stadium to the Metallica song "Enter Sandman" at every

game. To start each home game at Florida State University, the home of the Seminoles, Chief Osceola rides "Renegade" the horse around the field. Chief Osceola then dashes to the center of the field and plants a flaming spear into the ground. The University of Oklahoma school mascot is a replica of a 19th-century covered wagon, called the "Sooner Schooner." When the OU football team scores, the Sooner Schooner is pulled across the field by a pair of horses named "Boomer" and "Sooner." There is another grand college football tradition that involves a live animal mascot, a female bison named — Ralphie The Buffalo.

Ralphie the Buffalo is the name of the mascot of the University of Colorado Buffaloes. The team of "Ralphie Handlers," who are varsity student-athletes, run Ralphie around Folsom Field, the University of Colorado's football field, in a horse shoe pattern before each half of every home game. It takes five Ralphie Handlers to run her around the field: two up front on each side to steer her around the field, two in the back on each side to help guide her, and one in far back to control her speed, called the "loop" position. The tradition began in 1934. Football players have traditions too. At Harvard University, since 1884, a little red flag is carried by the player on the team who has played in the most Harvard vs. Yale games. He remains the flag keeper until he graduates and passes the flag down to the next player in succession.

While the game of football began with the Ivy League colleges such as Princeton University and Columbia University, the popularity of the game spread across the country quickly. In 1889, the University of Wisconsin started their football program and played their first game. With a football program as old as Wisconsin's, they have some the oldest and best football traditions.

On the morning of gameday in Wisconsin's capital city of Madison, the city hosts a farmer's market that surrounds the beautiful state capitol building. The farmer's market is a tradition, but so is the way the people walk around. Everyone walks together around the state capitol, counterclockwise. Hours before the game, students and alumni gather on campus at the lakeshore and enjoy food and drinks together. At the same time, a pep rally is held at the student union with cheerleaders and the marching band on the other side of campus. As it gets close to game time, the students and alumni walk together to the football stadium known as Camp Randall. During the game, there are so many team chants and songs that the university has another tradition called "Welcome Week" where the incoming freshmen are taught all the school rituals and traditions. Some of the traditions revolve around the school mascot — Bucky the Badger.

Bucky the Badger is certainly a crowd favorite. Bucky becomes the most popular individual in the stadium after the home team scores a touchdown. The mascot does push-ups after every touchdown. Bucky does a push-up for each point scored, cumulatively after a score. If the Badgers are up 7–0 and they score again, Bucky does seven push-ups, then seven more for the previous points scored. Over in the student section, there is another tradition taking place throughout the game as upperclassmen and underclassmen from the sections of 'P" and "O" chant back and forth at each other throughout the entire game, usually yelling profanities at their fellow classmates. For sure, the most popular football game tradition at Wisconsin takes place in between the third and fourth quarter. If the fans by chance are getting tired or cold, the tradition called "Jump Around" is sure to help. Since the tradition began in 1988, the song "Jump Around" by House of Pain is played and the fans jump up and down like hot popcorn seeds. The stadium literally shakes and by the time the song is over, the devoted fan base is ready for the final quarter of play, pumped up and ready to root on their home team. After the game, win or lose, fans stay in the stadium for another tradition called — Bucky's Fifth Quarter. Wisconsin's marching band plays fan favorites like "On Wisconsin," "Tequila," and "Hey Baby." Wisconsin has some great football traditions, but there might be at least one other university that can outdo them, and that is — The University of Notre Dame.

The football traditions at the University of Notre Dame are renowned in the religion of football. The football program hosts a pep rally the night before their home games, and at midnight on Fridays, the Notre Dame drumline gathers in the front of the Basilica of the Sacred Heart ring on campus and performs for the faithful team supporters. Of course, fans tailgate on gameday, but the university also offers their students and alumni multiple opportunities to attend a public mass before and even after football games. In addition, the football team gathers for a private team mass in the Basilica before each home game. After the team mass, the Notre Dame players walk together through campus to the football stadium. As the players make their way to the locker room, they are surrounded by thousands of students who wish the players good luck before they represent their university and take the field. The students follow the players into the stadium and they stand in the student section throughout the game. Before the Notre Dame players leave their locker room and enter the tunnel on to the field, they each slap a sign above their heads that reads "Play Like a Champion Today."

During the game, the Notre Dame fans have their own traditions inside the stadium such as dangling their car keys in the air on important plays. After the game, the Notre Dame players stand in front of the student section, locked arm in arm, and the band performs Notre Dame's alma mater, "Notre Dame, Our Mother." Speaking of the Notre Dame marching band, they also have their own traditions including always performing specific songs during the football games such as the "1812 Overture" and the Darth Vader theme music from the movie *Star Wars*. Notre Dame and Wisconsin both have several renowned, time-honored football traditions, but there is one tradition in college football that may please the Football Gods almost as much as coaches and players praying together. This tradition involves a children's hospital and a college football stadium. It's called — The Iowa Wave.

At Kinnick Stadium, the home of the Iowa Hawkeyes, at the end of the first quarter, all 60,000 plus fans turn and face the University of Iowa Stead Family Children's Hospital, which directly overlooks the stadium, and together they wave to patients and their families watching the game from the hospital. Everyone in the stadium, including the public address announcer, join the wave. This could be the best tradition in college football. Perhaps this tradition brings good luck because since Iowa fans began the tradition of "The Wave" in 2017, the team is 24–7 in home games.

National Football League teams have not been around as long as most college football programs, but they also have plenty of their own traditions. In Tampa Bay for example, Raymond James Stadium, the home of the Buccaneers, has a life-size pirate ship in the north end of the stadium. After the home team scores a touchdown or kicks a field goal, the pirate ship fires shots out of a cannon. In New England, the Patriots have employees dressed up like Revolutionary War soldiers and they fire muskets after every home team touchdown. In Seattle, the Seahawks retired the uniform number "12" to honor their loyal fans as their "12th man on the field." Before each home game, a sports celebrity raises the 12th man flag.

The Las Vegas Raiders have a section known as "The Black Hole" where the fans dress in silver and black and wear freaky and scary costumes that are gothic and evil looking. Many fans are outfitted as Darth Vader, a vampire, or a skeleton-looking character clothed in a Raiders uniform and helmet. In Cleveland, the stadium has a section called "The Dog Pound" and all the fans wear masks of dogs. In Pittsburgh, the Steelers fans wave a gold-colored towel throughout the entire game called a "Terrible Towel." In Kansas City, the Chiefs have several football traditions such as inviting a celebrity to bang the war drum before the game. On big plays, fans of the Chiefs do the increasingly controversial "Tomahawk Chop." The action involves moving the forearm forwards and backwards repetitively with an open palm to simulate a Native American tomahawk chopping. Chiefs fans also do a one-time tomahawk chop after the home team earns a first down.

The players and coaches of the football games may change, but the traditions remain the same. Traditions bring a feeling of pride and comfort. They keep us connected to the past and help football fans of the same team join together in solidarity. Football fanatics of the same team are unified by their traditions and they also unite together against their rivals.

CHAPTER SEVEN

The Rivalries

"An atheist is a man who watches a Notre Dame–Southern Methodist
University game and doesn't care who wins."
—Dwight D. Eisenhower

A RIVALRY, BY DEFINITION, IS THE STATE OF TWO
people or groups engaging in a lasting competitive relation-
ship. Each participant or side is a rival to the other. When
a rivalry becomes intense and vengeful, a team's main rival
is called an "archrival." In order for a rivalry to persist,
the competition on the field must be fierce for the football players to continue with a spirit of angst against each
other. Rivalries do not just exist in the religion of football.
Rivalries go back to biblical times.

In the book *The Baseball Gods are Real–Vol. 3: The
Religion of Baseball*, baseball fanatics were compared to
religious zealots. The "Zealots" were a political movement
depicted in the Bible, which sought to incite the people
of Judea to rebel against the Roman Empire and expel it
from the Holy Land by force of arms during time of the

Jewish-Roman War (66–70 CE). The term "Zealot" means one who is vehement on behalf of God. The Zealots had critics in their time as some people felt they were unwilling to compromise and had blind faith in their militaristic goals. The Zealots were obsessed with freedom and liberty and believed that God was to be their only ruler and lord. The religious zealots of Judea were adversaries with the Roman Empire back in ancient times just as football teams rival each other today.

The Buffalo Bills are usually voted the "best fans" in the National Football League. Despite the very cold weather in Buffalo, fans fill up their stadium for every home game and tailgate with the best of them, no matter how cold or snowy the weather might be. Bills fans get most pumped up to face off against their rivals which include the New York Jets and the New England Patriots.

The Green Bay Packers have passionate fans who get most excited to face off against their rivals such as the Minnesota Vikings and the Chicago Bears. The New York Giants have loyal fans who can't wait each season to defeat their rivals such as the Dallas Cowboys and the Philadelphia Eagles. The long-suffering Cleveland Browns fans have supported their team despite so many disappointing seasons. But even when the Browns are last in the division, the supporters get excited to face off against their divisional rivals such as the Pittsburg Steelers and Baltimore Ravens.

When football teams play against each other often or are located in close proximately to each other, the players and coaches, and their loyal fans tend develop contentions. When disputes, disagreements, jealousy, and bitterness between two National Football League teams and their fans reach a high enough threshold, a new rivalry is born. The same is true in college football. Some of the best college football rivalries include Army vs. Navy, Alabama vs. Auburn, Michigan vs. Ohio State, Oklahoma vs. Texas, USC vs. Notre Dame, Florida vs. Florida State, Harvard vs. Yale, California vs. Stanford, Indiana vs. Purdue, Wisconsin vs. Minnesota, Oregon vs. Oregon State, Tulane vs. LSU, BYU vs. Utah, Arizona vs. Arizona State, Duke vs. North Carolina, UCLA vs. USC, South Carolina vs. Clemson, Oklahoma vs. Oklahoma State, Georgia vs. Georgia Tech, Penn State vs. Pittsburg, Iowa vs. Iowa State, Mississippi State vs. Mississippi and Colorado vs. Colorado State.

Well-known stories of sibling rivalries in the Bible include the story of Cain vs. Abel, Jacob vs. Esau, and Joseph vs. his brothers. The lesson in these biblical stories is that while rivals see themselves as "against another," God sees us all as his children, without favoritism.

CHAPTER EIGHT

The Superstitions and Rituals

"Having gone through the experience of losing 31 straight games–24 of them being in charge–I think I've probably tried every single ritual that could possibly exist."
—Jay Civetti

THERE IS A SUBTLE BUT IMPORTANT DIFFERENCE between a superstition and a ritual. A superstition is any belief that is considered to be supernatural in nature. Superstitions can be beliefs about specific activities or things such as an object that brings good luck or wards off bad luck. A ritual is a spiritual activity always done in a particular situation and in the same way each time. Superstitions and rituals go hand in hand in the religion of football.

In November of 2021, writer Chris Blake penned an article for the *Columbia Missourian* about a high school football coach and his team's superstitions and rituals called "From Sonic to marbles: Inside Jefferson City football's superstitions." According to the story, Jefferson High School football head coach Damon Wells was going for a walk with his wife when he came across a black marble. The coach thought it was strange to find a black marble seemingly in the middle of nowhere on their walk. He decided to pick up the black marble and put it in his pocket.

The black marble was in Coach Wells' pocket when his team defeated Smith-Cotton High School a few days later, so he kept the marble in his pocket. The next week, his team won again. And they won again the week after that! The Jefferson High School Jays had a record of 0–3 before the marble and they were 6–1 since the marble, landing them in the Class 4 District 5 Final! It turns out that Coach Wells was not the only superstitious person affiliated with the football team.

Hayden Wells, Coach Damon Wells' son, is the team's starting quarterback. On game days, Hayden eats the same meal every time: an egg, pepper jack cheese, and Canadian bacon sandwich on an English muffin. Hayden also has another food ritual on game day, which he started with his grandma during his freshman year. He drives to Sonic for a chicken sandwich or a double cheeseburger. Hayden Wells is not the only player with game-day superstitions and rituals on his high school football team. According to sports-writer Chris Blake, Brody Smith, Hayden's teammate, eats two Snickers on game days, one before the game and one at halftime. He's been doing this ritual since the eighth grade. Perhaps it was not a coincidence that the Jefferson High School Jays turned around a four-season losing streak after the team fully embraced their superstitions and rituals. Maybe Coach Damon Wells had learned about how superstitions and rituals helped Tufts University's football program turn around their team's trajectory and change their fate.

Tufts University for years had one of the worst performing college football programs in the country. The Tufts football team went winless with a 0–8 record three years a row in 2011, 2012, and 2013 after going 1–7 in 2010. In 2014, the Tufts Jumbos started to win a few games every season and by 2016, the program had emerged with a terrific 7–1 record, good enough for second place in the New England Small College Athletic Conference. Curious as to how the Tufts football program managed to turn things around after all those years, student reporter Sam Weitzman found out that the secret to the team's success may have been that the players had become superstitious.

The Tufts Daily Sportswriter Sam Weitzman, wrote in his article "The reasons for rituals: the logic behind football superstitions," that senior linebacker Zach Thomas cleans his ears with cotton swab Q-Tips before every game. Sophomore wide receiver Winton Blount washes his hands multiple times before a game. Sophomore running back Jay Taylor completes exactly 32 push-ups before he takes the field, and junior offensive lineman Dan Dewing listens to "Baba O'Riley," by the British rock icons The Who. Senior defensive back J.P. Garcia wears a red wristband on his left arm, while sophomore linebacker Greg Holt always wears a bracelet on his right wrist. Kicker/punter Matthew Alswanger goes out onto the field before everyone and takes a lap around the track. Sportswriter Sam Weitzman suggests that the Tufts football players became superstitious and ritualistic after watching their own head coach. Tufts football head coach Jay Civetti told Weitzman, "Having gone through the experience of losing 31 straight games–24 of them being in charge–I think I've probably tried every single ritual that could possibly exist." Coaches and players are not just superstitious and ritualistic at the high school and college level, they are also this way in the National Football League.

While New York Jets running back Curtis Martin was famous for reading the Bible before every game, most of the renowned rituals amongst National Football League players are related to food. Famous retired Chicago Bears linebacker Michael Urlacher was well known for eating chocolate chip cookies on game day. Davante Adams, superstar wide receiver for the Las Vegas Raiders, eats salmon salad before each game. He's been doing that meal routine since his rookie season.

The most superstitious and ritualistic football player in the National Football League over the years may have been Seattle Seahawks power running back Marshawn Lynch. Since he was a little kid, Lynch would eat Skittles candy during his games. When he would score an NFL touchdown, Seattle Seahawks fans would throw Skittles on to the field. Now retired, in 2020, Lynch was interviewed by Peyton Manning in an episode of *Peyton's Places*. Lynch admitted to Manning that he actually had another pregame ritual besides eating Skittles. Lynch told Manning that before each game he would take a shot of Hennessy, the world's most popular cognac.

It's not just the National Football League players, it's the coaches as well. For example, the wife of Washington

Commanders head coach Ron Rivera makes him home-made cookies before each game, peanut butter and oatmeal. Stephanie Rivera also makes her husband the same breakfast on game day, cinnamon toast and ham. It should be noted that not all NFL head coaches have superstitions and rituals. In 2017 during a press conference, New England Patriots head coach Bill Belichick was asked if he had any superstitions, rituals or a pre-game routine. His mundane reply, "Yeah. I try to coach and play good."

CHAPTER NINE

The Freak Injuries

"The thing about football, the important thing about football, is that it is not just about football."
—Terry Pratchett

WARNING: IF YOU ARE AN ACTIVE FOOTBALL PLAYER at any level, you may not want to read this chapter. Seriously, you just might want to skip it. Since our thoughts can manifest in our physical reality, I don't think it's a good idea for your mind to focus on this chapter's subject matter, not even for one second. For retired athletes and regular folks, I hope you find this chapter interesting and thought provoking. And on second thought, if you are an active football player who has been getting injured a lot recently, in strange ways, perhaps you really should read this chapter. In fact, you probably should read it very carefully.

It seems that an effective way for the Football Gods to get the attention of an athlete is with an injury. If a player is not getting the message, the Football Gods may increase the number and intensity of the injuries and, to make a point, may cause the injuries to happen in an unusual manner. When these bizarre, debilitating, and painful events occur in football, they are called — Freak Injuries. The history of freak injuries in football is long and well documented. Sometimes injuries happen on the field. Other times, they happen elsewhere. There is a possibility that they may occur as part of an elaborate scheme built into the fabric of the universe by the Football Gods, possibly to help enforce the laws of karma. In this manner, they help souls living as humans on this planet to grow and evolve through adversity. When the Football Gods see a football player making poor life decisions and veering in the wrong direction on his or her life path, hidden forces in the universe may intervene.

If the universe is designed to keep a person's karma in balance, an injury can be used as an effective tool to help make this happen. However, when the universe really needs to get an athlete's attention, a simple, common injury, like a mild muscle strain, might be not enough. To get a football player to recognize that the Football Gods are trying to send a serious message or a warning, the injury may need to be freakier or more severe. If the injury is sufficiently severe or freaky, it just may make the athlete more responsive and introspective.

Visualize an athlete lying in bed with a cast on his or her leg from a recent injury. Now there is time to contemplate life and revisit past actions. If the injury is serious, the athlete likely will think about what life would be like without the ability to play the sport he or she loves so much. When an athlete has something taken away, like participating in that sport, he or she may search his or her soul and decide to do whatever it takes to makes things right. Typically, after recovering from such a serious injury, an athlete becomes grateful, humbled, and yes, somehow better and stronger for having gone through and learned from the experience. For example, who could ever forget the freak injury incident that took place with the Jacksonville Jaguars and their head coach, Jack Del Rio. The freak incident is now infamous and has earned itself a nickname — The Keep Chopping Wood Incident.

In 2003, after a 0–3 start to their season, Jaguars head coach Jack Del Rio came up with an idea that he hoped would fire up his team and inspire them to get out of their losing streak. He came up with the slogan "Keep Chopping Wood" as a reference to hard work and persistence. He took the metaphor literally and brought an ax and a log of wood into the team locker room. Del Rio took a hack at the wood with the ax and then encouraged his players to each have a turn "chopping the wood" as their teammates and coaches cheered them on. Coach Del Rio must have felt proud of himself as the idea seemed popular amongst the players and they were indeed getting pumped up and inspired. However, when punter Chris Hanson took his turn with the heavy, sharp ax, he accidentally missed the wood stump with his ax swing and cut himself in his right leg! Hanson was rushed to the hospital and the leg injury ended his season. A freak injury indeed! In recent years, there have also been examples of freak injuries at the college level.

In October of 2020, an article written by Andrew Schnitker was titled, "UT receiver Jordan Whittington sidelined for several weeks with 'freak' injury." According to

the article, Jordan Whittington, a talented redshirt freshman, had a freak injury that would keep him out of action
for several weeks as his injured hip flexor strain healed.
The injury must have been pretty freaky because Texas
Longhorns head coach Tom Herman refused to disclose
how the injury happened. A year later, three more freak
injuries would occur on the college football scene.

In March of 2021, Texas A&M star tight end Jalen
Wydermyer suffered a freak injury from an off the field accident. Aggies head coach Jimbo Fisher would not disclose
how the injury happened, but he did say that the injury was
significant enough that surgery would be required to repair
Wydermyer's cut tendon on one of his fingers. A few months
later, in August of 2021, LSU quarterback Myles Brennan
broke his arm during a freak accident. Myles had fishing
gear in his hands when his flip flop got caught in the deck,
causing him to fall. It turns out Myles fractured a bone in
his left arm as he tried to break his fall. Then, in November
of 2021, Florida Gators quarterback Anthony Richardson
suffered a concussion and an injured knee the night before
their game at South Carolina. How did Richardson get
hurt? He was practicing a dance move. While the bad injuries that happened to the above-mentioned football players
were freaky, there is nothing quite as freaky in the religion
of football as — The Ghosts.

CHAPTER TEN

The Ghosts

"That's one for the Gipper."
—Jack Chevigny

YES INDEED, JUST LIKE IN THE RELIGION OF BASEBALL, the religion of football does have tales and legendary stories about ghosts. By definition, a ghost is a soul of a dead person believed to be an inhabitant of the unseen world or to appear to be living in bodily likeness. In mythology and folklore, most ghosts are portrayed as a "vengeful spirit" of a dead person who returns from the afterlife to seek revenge for a cruel, unnatural, or unjust death.

ESPN sportswriter Ryan McGee penned an article in October 2021 called "College football's most vexing curses, from haunted Heismans to graveside gridirons." McGee writes:

> Take, for instance, The Citadel in Charleston, South Carolina. The military school that has long played in the FCS Southern Conference has won only four

league titles since joining the SoCon ranks in 1936. The first two came in 1961 and 1992. Over the next half-dozen years after that second title, a number of bodies were discovered around the area of Johnson Hagood Stadium, first beneath a room where boosters gathered before Bulldogs home games, then under the parking lot. Archaeologists and historians eventually uncovered the remains of nearly 350 people throughout the stadium grounds.

While Ryan McGee did not report that any students had seen ghosts around Hagood Stadium in recent years, that is not the case near the surrounding areas of Camp Randall Stadium at the University of Wisconsin. As legend has it, long before the stadium was built, the land was a training ground for Union soldiers during the Civil War. To make it a bit freakier, there also used to be a prison for Confederate soldiers nearby. Some Wisconsin Badgers fans may question how many beers they had to drink during the tailgate party because students and alumni over the years have claimed to see ghosts of Confederate soldiers wandering outside and inside the stadium. The ghostly soldiers are said to still look wounded from battle, wearing slings and bandages for their injuries. Need more proof that football ghosts are real?

There is the legendary spooky story involving a football ghost at the University of Notre Dame. According to the College Football Hall of Fame:

Our story begins on the Notre Dame campus on

a cold, pitch-black night in December 1920. After a late night out celebrating his final football game against Northwestern University, George Gipp missed curfew and found the doors to his dormitory, Washington Hall, locked. Rather than sneak in and risk getting caught, he decided to sleep outside. This decision likely led to his death as he contracted pneumonia and later died from complications. Not long after Gipp's death, the students who lived in Washington Hall started to experience signs of a paranormal visitor. They reported hearing strange noises, like papers rustling under doors, music being played late at night, phantom footsteps and even horns going off without warning. Gipp's spirit lives on through football, as his story is one of the many Notre Dame football legends passed down over the years. On his death bed, Gipp made this famous plea to coach Knute Rockne, "I've got to go, Rock. It's all right. I'm not afraid. Some time, Rock, when the team is up against it, when things are wrong and the breaks are beating the boys, tell them to go in there with all they've got and win just one for the Gipper. I don't know where I'll be then, Rock. But I'll know about it, and I'll be happy." From that moment on, Rockne used the story of the Gipper to rally the Fighting Irish. In the 12–6 upset of the previously undefeated Army team in 1928, Jack Chevigny, Notre Dame halfback, scored the tying touchdown at Yankee Stadium where he said, "That's one for the Gipper."

One more legendary story about football ghosts needs to be shared before we move to the next chapter and it takes place in the state of Kansas. A spooky, paranormal legend still lingers in the hearts and minds of football fanatics on the campus of Kansas State University in Manhattan, Kansas. As the story goes, a ghost named Nick haunts the Purple Masque Theatre, which is housed inside the enclosed stands of East Stadium. After the football stadium was built in the 1950s, a football player suffered a freak injury and died on campus before making it to the hospital. The ghost of East Stadium is reported to make noises, shuffle boxes and chairs, play music, make wooden boxes levitate, and even discharge the fire extinguisher! No doubt the football zealots at the University of Wisconsin, the University of Notre Dame, and Kansas State University would agree that football ghosts are real.

CHAPTER ELEVEN

The Curse of the Kansas City Chiefs

"I'm outta here so we can get the second-half comeback going.
I gotta leave, man. It's the only hope."
—Charles "Bad Luck Chuck" Penn

A CURSE IS AN INVOCATION THAT BRINGS SOME FORM
of adversity, misfortune, harm, or injury to a person. A
curse can also befall a place or an object. A curse is supernatural in nature and is considered to be made effective by
a spiritual power from a god, a spirit, or a demon. A curse
can also be conjured by a black magician or witch who uses
rituals to craft a spell to curse someone or something. In the
religion of football, a curse, also known as a "hex," can be
broken with rituals or prayer, but until a curse is broken, it
is often used to explain the failures or misfortunes of sports
teams and even specific players.

Back in 2012, a growing number of Kansas City sports
fans became convinced that their beloved Chiefs football
team was cursed. In late October of 2012, a discussion
board called *Chiefs Planet* had a chat room named "The

Lounge" and a topic posted for discussion was titled, "Is Arrowhead Cursed?" A chat room member with the tag name "kushedgod" started off the discussion with the comment, "This stadium looks so evil and depressing and I heard Arrowhead was built on an Indian burial ground, true or not?" Chat room member "Phobia" responded, "Indeed. Arrowhead is cursed. That explains why the Chiefs look like shit at home and do so well on the road." Referring to the Chiefs' former general manager, "I hear Carl Peterson is living in Sauer Castle and performing witchcraft daily to keep the curse going." Referring to the Chiefs' current GM hired in 2009, a chat room member named "Bump" wrote: "Arrowhead isn't cursed. Scott Pioli is." Then "kushedgod" got back into the online conversion, writing, "Arrowhead is cursed. The whole franchise is." To end the discussion on the board, "memyselfI" wrote, "Not just Arrowhead, I think the entire Truman Sports Complex. I wish they would torch those facilities and start fresh someplace else. Too much bad mojo." Mojo is defined as an ability or quality that causes one to excel or have good luck. Die-hard Chiefs fans were not the only ones claiming the team was cursed, as sportswriters felt the same way.

Writing for the *Bleacher Report*, sportswriter Brandon Alisoglu penned an article in 2012 called "Kansas City Chiefs: Awful or Cursed?" In his editorial, however, Alisoglu concludes that the team was not cursed by a demon or a vengeful ghost but rather cursed by "scouting ineptitude and terrible play." Sportswriter Aiken Drum wrote an article for *Fanpost* with the name "Is There a Curse on the Chiefs?" The *Fanpost* commentary concluded that poor gameplay surely has contributed to several first-round play-off losses over the years, but according to Drum, it came down to "bad juju."

Juju, or ju-ju, is a spiritual belief system incorporating objects, such as amulets and spells used in religious practice in traditional African religions. In general terms, "juju" can be used to refer to magical properties dealing with good luck. Those well versed in the religion of football have reverence for the spiritual energy that comes with the term "juju." Perhaps that is why Kansas City Chiefs wide receiver John Sherman Smith-Schuster goes by the nickname "JuJu."

In 2013, things started to turn around for the cursed Kansas City Chiefs with the hiring of veteran head coach Andy Reid. Over the next five seasons, Reid's Chiefs became one of the best teams in the league. The Chiefs were 11–5 in 2013, 9–7 in 2014, 11–5 in 2015, 12–4 in 2016, 10–6 in 2017, and 12–4 in 2018. All winning seasons, including back-to-back AFC West division titles in 2016 and 2017. The curse chatter quieted down for several seasons until a new curse thesis emerged since despite the Chiefs' success since 2013, the team had not won a home playoff game. Many loyal fans wondered if the Chiefs had a home playoff curse.

The Chiefs lost at home in the Wild Card round in 2013. In 2015, they lost at home in the Divisional Playoff round. In 2016, Kansas City lost again at home in the Divisional Playoff Round. And then again in 2017, the Chiefs failed to earn a home playoff win and were knocked out of the playoffs in the Wild Card Round on their home turf. In 2018, the Chiefs made it all the way to the AFC Championship but lost at home to Bill Belichick and his New England Patriots in overtime. After another successful season that ended with a disappointing playoff defeat, the curse chatter in Kansas City reemerged. Kansascity.com ran a story with the headline, "Is Arrowhead Jinxed?" Several loyal Chiefs supporters were now convinced that the team was cursed and a few brave fans decided to do something about it.

Two die-hard Chiefs fans, Gary McKenzie and Anthony Stratton, who operate a fan discussion board called *Arrowhead Guys*, took a tour of Arrowhead Stadium. They brought with them a psychic medium named Vicky Millard from Topeka, Kansas, to help them get rid of what they believed to be "negative energy" around the team and its home stadium. As they walked together around the empty, quiet stadium, Vicky Millard came in contact with the ghost of former Chiefs Super Bowl winning head coach Hank Stram, who died in 2005.

Vicky Millard said that Coach Stram was wearing a suit from the early 1970s and suspected that the ghost of Hank Stram had been haunting the Chiefs ever since he passed away. She said it was because he was fired, which he considered disrespectful and an insult since he helped the team win their first Super Bowl. Stram was fired in 1974 and the Chiefs had not won a home playoff game since. After telepathically communicating with the ghost of Hank Stram, the medium recommended that Chiefs fans show more appreciation of Coach Stram at the next home game. She said that if they did it with enough love and respect, the curse might be lifted. Before the group left Arrowhead

Stadium, they walked onto the field and stopped at the 50-yard line in the center of the stadium. Together, they made a blessing and said a prayer, asking for the Chiefs' playoff curse to be lifted.

In 2019, under Andy Reid's leadership, the Kansas City Chiefs had another terrific season, finishing first in the division with a 12–4 record. The Chiefs' first playoff game against the Houston Texans would be held at Arrowhead Stadium. The game got off to a terrible start for the home Kansas City Chiefs and before the fans could blink their eyes, their beloved Chiefs were already losing 24–0! The Texans were 5–0 during the season after leading by 14 points or more at any point. This was the largest deficit of the season for the Chiefs. While Chiefs fans such as Gary McKenzie and Anthony Stratton thought for sure they had done the necessary spiritual work with psychic medium Vicky Millard, it turns out that there was one more "bad luck hex" that needed to be removed from the stadium. That bad luck jinx was not an object, but actually a person named Charles Penn, and this superstitious, die-hard Kansas City Chiefs fan even had a nickname — Big Buck Chuck.

Lifelong Chiefs fan Charles Penn, a 31-year-old postal clerk, spent $258 for his Chiefs home game playoff ticket. When the Chiefs were losing 21–0, Penn posted a video of himself on social media claiming that he was bad luck and his presence at Arrowhead Stadium had jinxed his favorite team. Penn tweeted, "I'm outta here so we can get the second-half comeback going. I gotta leave, man. It's the only hope." The Chiefs' fortunes turned as soon as he left the building. Penn's video went viral and received more than a million views. Big Buck Chuck had just earned himself a new nickname — Bad Luck Chuck.

Bad Luck Chuck got home and watched the playoff game on his television. As Chuck viewed the game from his living room, Kansas City scored 42 unanswered points and went on to defeat Houston by 20 points, one of the biggest comebacks in NFL history. After the game, the Twitter universe went off dropping tons of amazing statistics from the epic Chiefs' comeback home playoff victory. This was only the second time all season an NFL team had fallen behind by 21 points in the first quarter. Since falling behind 24–0, the Chiefs had seven consecutive touchdown drives. At one point during the second half, the Chiefs had scored 51 points in just 32 minutes of gameplay. Travis Kelce had 10 catches, setting a new franchise record for catchers in a single game, and he also became the third tight end in NFL history to score three touchdowns in a playoff game. Patrick Mahomes became the ninth and youngest QB to have 300 yards passing and five TDs in a playoff game. The Chiefs became the first team in NFL history, regular season or playoffs, to trail by 24-plus points in the first half and be tied or leading entering halftime. During the postgame press conference, Bad Luck Chuck's story was mentioned, and when Chiefs quarterback Patrick Mahomes was asked if he had any advice for Charles Penn, he said, "Watch the next game at home." Bad Luck Chuck did indeed watch the next Chiefs playoff game at home.

Before the next game, which was the AFC Championship, Bishop James Johnston, who leads the Catholic Diocese of Kansas City-St. Joseph, had a chance to meet with Pope

Francis. At the meeting, Bishop Johnston presented Pope Francis with a signed Patrick Mahomes jersey. Pope Francis was grateful for the gift and had a big smile on his face as he held the jersey in his hands. No confirmation if Pope Francis said a prayer or gave a blessing to the jersey or the Kansas City Chiefs that day, but, sure enough, just like the week prior, the Kansas City Chiefs fell behind the Tennessee Titans 17–7, then staged another epic comeback to win the game. Then again, facing the San Francisco 49ers in the Super Bowl, the Chiefs managed to come back after trailing 20–10, to win their first Super Bowl in 50 years. Chiefs head coach Andy Reid won his second Super Bowl ring, coaching in his 222nd game on 2/2/2020.

In the days that followed the Kansas City Chiefs' epic Super Bowl victory, sportswriters were eager to write articles about "Bad Luck Chuck" and "The Playoff Curse" that was broken during the 2019–2020 NFL season. Leigh Oleszczak penned an article for *Fansided* called "Kansas City Chiefs: The Playoff Curse is Finally Broken," and over at *The Turf,* sportswriter Sydney Van Gorp published an article titled, "KC's 25 Year Playoff Curse is Broken." There was actually another curse that was broken the night the Chiefs won the 2019 Super Bowl — The Madden Curse.

Back in 2014, *Sports Illustrated* ran an article which highlighted the football players that were featured on the cover of the popular football video game called *Madden NFL.* Almost every player that had appeared on the video game cover incurred an injury during the season. Football players that fell victim to the "Madden Curse" included Eddie George in 2001, Daunte Culpepper in 2002, Michael

Vick in 2004, Ray Lewis in 2005, Donovan McNabb in 2006, Shaun Alexander in 2007, Vince Young in 2008, Brett Favre in 2009, Larry Fitzgerald and Troy Polamalu in 2010, Drew Brees in 2011, Peyton Hillis in 2012, Adrian Peterson in 2014, Oden Beckham, Jr. in 2016, and Rob Gronkowski in 2017. While there have been a few football players that have avoided injury after being featured on the cover of the game, such as Tom Brady in 2018, it was Chiefs quarterback Patrick Mahomes who officially broke the curse once and for all. While Mahomes did miss two games with an injured knee, he was able to recover and lead his team to a Super Bowl victory, the first Madden cover football player to do so.

Coming full circle, since head coach Andy Reid and star quarterback Patrick Mahomes joined the team, the Kansas City Chiefs have gone from cursed to blessed, but they have their amazing fans to thank for that. No doubt all the die-hard supporters in the Chiefs Kingdom would agree that football curses are real.

CHAPTER TWELVE

The Missionaries

"Some people think football is a matter of life and death. I don't like that attitude. I can assure them it is much more serious than that."
—Bill Shankly

A MISSIONARY IS A MEMBER OF A RELIGIOUS GROUP sent into an area to promote their faith or provide services, such as education, literacy, social justice, health care, or economic development. In the Bible, Jesus Christ used the word when sending his disciples to preach the gospel in his name. In the religion of football, the "missionaries" are the coaches, players, and team owners that make a discernable effort to give back to their communities with charity work and community service. Perhaps there is a correlation between charity work, community service, and success on the field. The Super Bowl winning Kansas City Chiefs would make a good case study.

Two days after they became champions of the National Football League in early February 2020, BBC News ran a headline, "Derrick Nnadi pays dog adoption fees after

Super Bowl Win." Nnadi's charitable giving is just a small example of the kind of giving back that Kansas City Chiefs players are doing all the time. When the Chiefs returned to the Super Bowl during the 2020–2021 season, Chiefs defensive star Tyrann Mathieu surprised an intensive care unit nurse with tickets to the big game. Mathieu said he wanted to do something special for someone working on the front lines during the COVID-19 pandemic. Nurse Brian Smith, who worked for Saint Luke's South in Overland Park, Kansas, said that he loved the Chiefs but had never been to an NFL game in his life.

During the 2021 season, Chiefs fan Louie Brewer was active on the Chiefs fan message boards, but when his fellow message board friends noticed that Brewer had not posted in the group chat for a few days, his friends went to his home and found him lying nearly dead on the floor. Brewer had suffered a stroke and had laid on the floor of his home suffering for five days before help arrived. Louie Brewer temporarily lost his ability to speak from the stroke. The first word out of his mouth after his medical incident was — Chiefs. When Kansas City wide receiver Tyreek Hill heard about Brewer's story, he paid him a visit in his rehabilitation facility. Hill gave Brewer a signed jersey and a hat with the understanding that Brewer would wear it to Arrowhead Stadium as soon as he was able. Kansas City Chiefs players are always looking out for opportunities to help people directly in the local community. The Kansas City Chiefs are also doing charity work and community service at the foundation level.

Kansas City tight end Travis Kelce and his "87 &

Running" foundation are empowering disadvantaged youth to achieve success by providing resources and support to their communities and cultivating their talent in the areas of education, business, athletics, and the arts. Tyrann Mathieu's foundation impacts the lives of financially disadvantaged children and youth through encouragement, opportunities, and resources to achieve their dreams in Kansas City and his hometown of New Orleans. In 2021, the Tyrann Mathieu Foundation helped pass out turkeys and Thanksgiving meals, drive-thru style, to local families as a part of his annual holiday giving event — Tyrann's Turkeys. The funds Mathieu has donated to The Giving Hope KC Food Pantry will provide Thanksgiving turkeys to 500 families. Then there is "15 and the Mahomies Foundation" led by Chiefs quarterback Patrick Mahomes. Dedicated to improving the lives of children, 15 and the Mahomies Foundation supports initiatives that focus on health, wellness, communities in need of resources, and other charitable causes. Kansas City Chiefs players keep giving back to their communities even after retirement.

Recently retired Chiefs fullback Anthony Sherman has joined Homeland Security Investigations (HSI) in the fight to end human trafficking. After 10 years in the National Football League, Sherman began a new career on the front lines of the law enforcement community by joining HSI Kansas City. Sherman is now working with law enforcement partners to combat the criminals that seek to exploit the nation's interstate systems, mail facilities, intermodal transportation, and general aviation routes that exist within the Kansas City area. The Chiefs players continue to give back, but so too does the Chiefs organization.

In September of 2021, Chiefs Kingdom raised more than $900,000 for Ronald McDonald House Charities of Kansas City by selling flags on "Red Friday." Over the past nine years, Red Friday sales have raised more than $3 million. Ronald McDonald house uses these funds to reduce the burden of childhood illness on children and their families by providing a "home away from home" while the children are receiving medical care in Kansas City area hospitals. The Kansas City Chiefs have a multitude of community outreach programs that focus on health and wellness. According to the team website:

Lift Up America – The Chiefs are partners with Lift Up America, and they have provided food to local communities for the past nine years. They annually give 60 area relief organizations 30,000 pounds of high protein food.

Chiefs Thanksgiving Food Distribution – Chiefs players, coaches, and staff have been collecting funds since 1992 to provide more than 18,200 families with food for Thanksgiving.

Operation Breakthrough Adopt-A-Family – Each year, the Chiefs Community Caring Team works with Operation Breakthrough's Holiday Adopt-A-Family program. The Chiefs help the center's families share a traditional holiday as a family unit.

Chiefs Blood Drive – The Chiefs host the Chiefs Blood

Drive each year during Thanksgiving Week to support local hospitals, patients, and physicians. The Kansas City Chiefs also partner with the Community Blood Center to increase the blood supply available for the 70+ hospital partners in Kansas and Missouri.

Souper Bowl of Caring – The Souper Bowl of Caring is held annually and works to fight food insecurity in local communities. The Chiefs are a national sponsor of the Souper Bowl of Caring hunger relief program, and their work in the program has helped provide more than 100,000 meals locally.

KC Chiefs Play 60 – The KC Chiefs, Chiefs Community Caring Team, help spread the NFL's Play 60 message by encouraging the youth to create healthy eating habits and exercising for at least 60 minutes each day.

Youth Football Outreach – The Chiefs are committed to providing access to football to young athletes. In the fall of 2008, they created a youth football field at the University of Kansas Hospital Training Complex through funding from the Hunt Family Foundation and the NFL Youth Football Funding Board. Located close to the Chiefs Practice Facility and Arrowhead Stadium, it has given youth in the area the opportunity to play football like their favorite NFL players. Almost 20,000 youth football players and coaches have been able to use the field, as it's home to various youth teams, leagues, and programs. The Chiefs and the NFL have also partnered and donated almost $2 million for metro-area field refurbishments and constructions that have helped local fields.

Chief's Charity Game – The Kansas City Chiefs host a charity game with the Kansas City community that raises money for children's charities in their local community. This charity game has taken place since 1985 and was created by Chiefs founder Lamar Hunt. The Chiefs Charity Game has raised more than $13.7 million, assisting over 125 charities each year.

My Cause My Cleats – Chiefs players wear custom footwear to raise awareness of charities important to them. Players and coaches participate, and many shoes are auctioned after the following game with proceeds going to the respective causes or charities.

The Hunt family, owner of the Kansas City Chiefs, also has their own charitable foundation. Created in 1983, The Hunt Family Foundation assists over 60 local youth agencies each year. The foundation has improved the lives of children in the Kansas City community and has been able to donate millions of dollars for youth health and wellness, fitness, and education initiatives.

This kind of missionary work in the religion of football is certainly not exclusive to the Kansas City Chiefs. There are high school, college and professional football teams all over the country doing significant charity work and community service. The critical takeaway from this chapter is that doing charity work and community service pleases the Football Gods and giving back to others is one of the most effective ways for a player or a team to create good karma for themselves.

CHAPTER THIRTEEN

The Reincarnation of the Tulane Green Wave

"This is a very important time in our community's history and we want to do everything we can to make a positive change."

—Willie Fritz

FOR THOSE UNFAMILIAR WITH THE CONCEPT OF karma, it is a belief system at the core of several world religions including Hinduism, Buddhism, Ayyavazhi, Sikhism, and Jainism. The law of karma states that the sum of a person's actions in this and previous states of existence determine his or her fate and future existences. In terms of spiritual development, karma encompasses all that a person has done, is doing, and will do. Karma is not about punishment or reward. It is energy created every time a person is kind to another being. However, it is also energy created whenever a person causes suffering or harm to another being. Individuals can create good karma by being honest and telling the truth, by helping others, by being kind and compassionate, by thinking positive thoughts, by doing yoga, by eating healthy, and by living a purposeful life. You can guess, I'm sure, how bad karma is created. An interesting case study of good karma in college football is the small private university tucked into the beautiful Garden District of New Orleans, Louisiana — Tulane University.

The Tulane Green Wave Football program has a storied history. The university was founded in 1834, and in 1902, the school's football team was created and played their first season. Tulane's football program came from humble beginnings. During first 20 years of the football program as an independent team, meaning that they did not belong to a specific conference, they had several losing seasons. In 1922, Tulane moved into the Southern Conference and in 1931, after a terrific 11–1 season, Tulane made it to their first ever bowl game — The Rose Bowl.

While Tulane did lose in its first and only Rose Bowl appearance, two years later, Tulane was invited to join the SEC (Southeastern Conference). During Tulane's "SEC Years," they started out as a dominant football team. During their first ten years in the conference, Tulane made it to the prestigious Sugar Bowl twice and won the Sugar Bowl in 1934 after Ted Cox's team posted a 10–1 record. Tulane made it into the Top #25 NCAA Rankings in 1948, 1949, 1950, and 1956. Something went wrong however in the early 1960s and Tulane turned back into a losing program. After nine consecutive losing seasons in the SEC, Tulane made a big decision that would impact their football program for decades to come. Tulane quit the Southeastern Conference!

A charter member of the Southeastern Conference, Tulane followed in the footsteps of Georgia Tech, which departed the SEC in 1964 to become independent. According to Tulane's president at the time, Herbert E. Longenecker, Tulane had become a "highly selective" university and the school was now attracting students from all around the country and not just from the southern states. As part of a nationwide admissions strategy, Tulane wanted more freedom to play opponents from a wider geographic region of the country. When asked about the big move, Tulane's football coach at the time, Tommy O'Boyle, was quoted as saying that he was sure the move could not do their team any harm and he was looking forward to playing a national schedule. This strategic decision did indeed help Tulane recruit even higher quality students from around the country, but for Tulane's football program, it was a death sentence. Two decades went by as Tulane's football program became lifeless because recruiting became much more difficult due to more stringent academic requirements.

In the early 1990s, the Tulane football program hired Buddy Teevens to become their new head coach and he essentially took on the role as "the undertaker." Under Teevens' watch, Tulane's football team was metaphorically in a coma. The Super Dome in New Orleans could hold more than 80,000 fans, yet sometimes less than 5,000 supporters came to watch the games. In 1994, after a 1–10 season, loyal Tulane football fans had lost almost all hope.

In 1996, Tulane made a smart move and joined Conference USA after spending four decades as an independent team. Two years later, Tulane's football team appeared to have come back from the dead and mustered perhaps its best season since 1931 in 1998, when head coach Tommy Bowden and dynamic quarterback Shaun King led the Green Wave to an undefeated 12–0 season and a victory in the Liberty Bowl. Sadly, for Tulane's faithful followers, Tommy Bowden left the team before the big bowl game to take a new job, and Tulane's football program went back into a coma in the years that followed. While Tulane did make a trip to the Hawaii Bowl under new head coach Chris Scelfo in 2002 after an 8–5 season, Tulane went another 10 years without a winning record.

In 2014, Tulane moved over to the American Conference but the program resembled a collection of zombies, as they only managed three wins in 2014 and 2015. But something big happened in December of 2015. Tulane's football program metaphorically reincarnated with the hiring of turnaround specialist head coach from Shawnee Mission, Kansas — Willie Fritz.

The Green Wave's new head Willie Fritz brought with him three decades of coaching experience including turning around college football programs such as Central Missouri and Sam Houston State. Fritz was charismatic and had magnetic enthusiasm. He had a clever coaching style and a unique playbook that favored the running game. However, Fritz also brought something else very important with him to Tulane — Good Karma.

Willie Fritz understood that the best way to create good juju for his new team was for the coaches and players to be active in charity work and community service. While it took him a few years to rebuild Tulane's football program, each season the team won more games than the year before. In 2018, Fritz led Tulane to its first bowl game since 2013, a share of the American Conference title, and just its sixth winning season in the last 37 years. With one of the best rushing attacks in the nation, Fritz guided Tulane to three straight bowl games. Tulane played and won the Cure Bowl in 2018, won the Armed Forces Bowl in 2019, and played in but lost the Famous Idaho Potato Bowl in 2020. Tulane's football program resurrection could be attributed to better recruited players and a new offensive and defensive scheme, but no doubt the Football Gods understand that the biggest reason Tulane's football program came back from the dead was the good karma the coaches and players created for themselves by helping their local community.

In 2020, Willie Fritz and his wife, Susan, announced financial contributions to United Way of Southern Louisiana. In addition, Tulane's football players announced a financial contribution to the Louisiana Power Coalition for Equity and Justice as well as United Way of Southeast Louisiana. The gifts from the Fritz family and the Tulane players went to United Way's United for Equity Fund, which focuses on enhancing education, economic mobility, and health as a means to ensure community residents have equitable access to a quality life. The Louisiana Power Coalition works with community members to provide them with information they need to find their voice and learn where and when to use it.

Also, during the 2020 season, Tulane players wore special team jerseys to support The Wave of Change organization in their nationally televised game against Southern Methodist University. The all-black jerseys featured the text "Wave of Change" on the back of the nameplate. The special wording represents the Green Wave's player-focused group that is committed to bringing awareness to injustices and inequalities facing society. No doubt the Football Gods took notice and were pleased.

In 2021, Tulane's football team partnered with Sustaining Our Urban Landscape (SOUL) to give back to the New Orleans community. The football team traveled to the lower ninth ward to assist in planting trees to bolster SOUL's mission. Former Tulane wide receiver Sorrell Brown helped organize the event. SOUL's mission is to drive a resilient and environmentally equitable New Orleans by reforesting their urban landscape by planting trees. The clusters of trees they plant stave off flooding, reduce pollution, improve community health, and provide beauty and shade. Tulane University's devotion to charity work and community service has not gone unnoticed by the NCAA (National Collegiate Athletic Association).

Tulane placed fifth in the nation in NCAA's Team Works Community Service Competition in 2021 after placing fourth in 2019. To finish in the top of the list once again for Tulane is remarkable, especially since students were displaced for several months first due to the COVID-19 pandemic, and again after a hurricane hit New Orleans. Among many numerous service initiatives, Green Wave student-athletes, including members of the football team, accumulated hours assisting with Excite All Stars Diversity and Leadership virtual workshops with Lake Forest Elementary Charter School, volunteering with United Through Sport, making cards for Cards for Hospitalized Kids, volunteering with the Power Coalition's "Power

Hour," organizing a Voter Registration Drive, hosting virtual Special Olympics practices, and virtually volunteering as English as a second language instructors and educational assistants at local schools and churches. With each act of giving back, these football missionaries at Tulane University are spreading love and light around the religion of football. By doing so, with every kind act, each individual builds up good karma for themselves and gets one step closer to becoming a saint.

CHAPTER FOURTEEN

The Saint

"As far as me and miracles, no... But in the God that we serve, yeah,
I do believe in miracles."
—Tim Tebow

IN RELIGIOUS BELIEF, A SAINT IS A PERSON WHO IS
recognized as having an exceptional degree of holiness,
likeness, or closeness to God. Depending on the religion,
saints are recognized either by official declaration as in the
Catholic faith, or by popular acclamation. In the religion
of Hinduism, it is believed that a saint can have certain
extraordinary miraculous powers. Hindus believe that
there is a "spiritual force field" that surrounds these highly
enlightened individuals. It is understood in yoga communities that gurus who achieve sainthood can touch the inner
lives of others in a transforming way. Saints are not believed
to have power on their own, but only that is granted by
God. In the religion of football, there is at least one bona
fide saint. His name is — Tim Tebow.

Tim Tebow was born in the Philippines to missionary parents who raised him to do exactly what Jesus taught his disciples to do, which was to be "fishers of men" and spread God's word by sharing their experiences with nonbelievers. A top recruit out of high school, Tebow attended college at the University of Florida. In his four years as a Florida Gator, Tebow emerged as one of the best college football players of all time. He led his football team to two national championships, and in 2007, he won the Heisman trophy for best player in the country. Along the way, Tebow became the face of evangelical Christians and a role model to millions of football fans.

After scoring a touchdown, which he did frequently during his college football days, Tim Tebow would kneel down in prayer. This ritual became known as — Tebowing. Tebow often used his football platform to share how important his faith was to him and he ended all of his interviews with "God bless." In 2009, during the national championship game, Tebow wore eye black under his eyes that read "John 3:16." During the game, more than 90 million people googled John 3:16, a passage from the Bible that says, "For God so loved the world that he gave his one and only son, that whoever believes in him shall not perish but have eternal life." After a remarkable college career at the University of Florida, Tebow was ready to play quarterback at the professional level in the National Football League.

The Denver Broncos selected Tim Tebow in the first round of the NFL draft in 2010. After injuries plagued the team, Tebow was promoted to starting quarterback in his second season. The Broncos had a 1–4 record, but some-how, Tebow turned the team around. The Broncos finished 8–8 and managed to sneak into the playoffs. Perhaps with the help of the Football Gods, Tim Tebow led his team to an overtime playoff victory against the highly favored Pittsburgh Steelers. This game became known as — The 3:16 Game.

The fingerprints left behind by the Football Gods during "The 3:16 Game" are nothing short of stunning. Tebow threw for 316 passing yards. Not only that, but Denver averaged 31.6 yards per reception as a team and the Broncos possessed the ball for 31:06 minutes. ESPN's ratings for the game, you guessed it — 3.16. To top it all off, hover-ing over the stadium throughout the 3:16 game was a lone cloud, shaped in the form of a halo. In various world reli-gions, a halo symbolizes sacred people.

After retiring from playing football, Tim Tebow went on to publish self-help books related to his spirituality and he spends lots of his time doing charity work and community service. However, after a brief career in sports broadcasting (which he picked up again later), Tebow returned to play-ing sports. However, rather than return to playing football, he decided to fulfill another lifelong dream of his and that was to play professional baseball. Tebow's baseball career was short, but it was miraculous.

On October 12, 2016, Tim Tebow made his debut as a baseball player for the New York Mets. After the game, a miracle took place. As described in an article written by Josh Peter on the same day, a fan suffered an apparent seizure while Tebow was signing autographs. Tebow went to the aid of the fan, put his hands on the man, and started praying. Shortly thereafter, the fan miraculously regained consciousness. In his first public comments about the incident, Tebow said, "As far as me and miracles, no…But in the God that we serve, yeah, I do believe in miracles." Tebow added, "I don't know what the situation was, but I know that the God that I get to serve is the God that is always performing miracles in people's lives every day, all the time. As a Christian, that's the hope that we get to live by…we get to serve a God that does amazing things every single day…It's one of the greatest hopes you get to live with."

This isn't even the first time Tim Tebow was credited with helping save a person's life. On June 26, 2016, while on a Delta Airlines flight, Tebow witnessed another medical emergency. A man was having heart problems and those around him feared he was having a heart attack. Tebow met the man's wife and led a prayer before the plane safety landed in Phoenix and the man was taken to the hospital.

Perhaps a miracle of lesser magnitude the next season, in Tim Tebow's first at bat he hit a two-run home run. That's right, the same guy who may have saved a man's life after a game in 2016 hit a home run during his first at bat of the 2017 season. Tebow led his new team, the South Carolina Fireflies, to a 14–7 victory over the visiting Augusta GreenJackets that afternoon. Journalist Ron Dicker's *Huffington Post* article regarding the game had the most fitting title: "Tim Tebow Homers in Minor League Season Debut, Miracles May Never Cease." Tim Tebow, keep doing what you are doing and may the Baseball Gods and the Football Gods always be with you!

CHAPTER FIFTEEN

The Sinners

"I deflate quicker than a terrible Patriots joke."
—Alison Hendricks

THE PREVIOUS CHAPTER CELEBRATED A FOOTBALL
saint. This chapter calls out the football sinners. In a religious context, a sin is a transgression against divine law. Each culture has its own interpretation of what it means to commit a sin. While sins are generally considered actions, any thought or word considered immoral, selfish, shameful, harmful, or alienating might be termed "sinful."

Football teams are always looking for an edge over their opponents. Maybe that is why coaches and players sometimes feel the need to cheat to gain a competitive advantage such as a wide receiver adding a foreign sticky substance to his gloves to improve his grip. As you would expect in the religion of football, there can be serious consequences for committing sins. Just go back and reread the chapters on curses and freak injuries. In the religion of football, every football team has cheated at one time or another.

There is literally a website called "Yourteamcheats. com" and they track all of the team and player rule violations and even keep grades! Their website tagline is, "So you think there's only one NFL team that cheats? You're wrong. All 32 NFL teams cheat." According to the website, even the curse-breaking Kansas City Chiefs have sinned in the religion of football. The Chiefs were caught cheating several times, including players taking performing-enhancing drugs, team executives tampering with the free-agent process and staff videotaping opposing teams' signals. In the National Football League, there have been three scandals that made the biggest headlines in recent years.

In the "Spygate" cheating scandal, the New England Patriots were caught illegally videotaping the signals used by the New York Jets coaching staff in a game in 2007. Yes, this was the same thing the Kansas City Chiefs were doing during the Marty Schottenheimer years. While the Chiefs may have learned their lesson and stopped sinning, the Patriots couldn't help themselves and in 2015, they were caught deliberately using deflated footballs in a win over the Colts in the AFC Championship game in 2015. A slightly deflated ball is a bit softer, making it easier for Patriots quarterback Tom Brady to grip the ball to throw it and reduces the bounce when it hits the hands of a receiver, making it easier to catch. That scandal earned itself a nickname as well, it was called — Deflategate. In both cases, the Patriots were punished by the league with financial fines and loss of draft picks.

New England Patriots head coach Bill Belichick was at it again in 2019. In 2020, it was discovered that during the previous season, the Patriots reached out to the Cleveland Browns for a credential for a videographer to shoot a behind-the-scenes piece on an advanced scout as part of their "Do Your Job" video series. Well, it turns out that the video crew did indeed film the Bengals coaching staff while in the press box at the Bengals–Browns game. The Patriots production team was barred from filming games during the 2020 season and paid a $1.1 million fine for filming the Bengals' sideline. The most egregious cheating scandal to take place in the NFL in recent memory involved the New Orleans Saints. The Saints got caught in a "bounty scandal" called — Bountygate.

The National Football League caught the New Orleans Saints paying out bonuses or "bounties" for injuring opposing team players. The pool was alleged to have been in operation from 2009 through 2011, which included the year 2009, the season the team won the Super Bowl. While player bounty systems have secretly been around NFL locker rooms for decades, what made the Saints' bounty program so egregious was that the program was run by the coaches. New Orleans head coach Sean Payton was suspended for the entire 2012 season and defensive coordinator Greg Williams was suspended indefinitely from the league.

While the New England Patriots are responsible for two of the biggest NFL cheating scandals in recent years, there appears to be evidence that the team has begun to pay off their bad karmic debt. In April of 2020, during the peak of the COVID-19 pandemic, the New England Patriots sent their team plane to Shenzhen, China, and purchased 1.2

million N95 masks. Patriots team owner, the Kraft family, paid $2 million, about half the costs to acquire the masks, and had them delivered directly to the practice facilities of the New York Jets, the team they spied on during the "Spygate" cheating scandal.

There have been cheaters at the college football level for decades. Who could forget the scandal at the University of North Carolina in Chapel Hill? Whistleblowers turned in the university because numerous football (and basketball) players over decades had benefited from taking fake courses. In recent years, football sinning continues to be discovered. In May of 2020, 24 football players for Army were caught in an academic cheating conspiracy.

In January of 2021, news broke about a recruiting scandal at the University of Tennessee. The school chancellor launched an internal investigation and what they discovered was "stunning." While the exact recruiting violations were never made public, many of the team's coaches were fired. For those wondering what Tennessee's football program did to violate recruiting rules, the recent scandal involving the football programs at the University of Georgia and the University of Alabama may provide a clue. In March of 2021, the Georgia Bulldogs and the Alabama Crimson Tide were both accused by a high school coach, who was caught on video alleging that both Georgia and Alabama paid top prospect high school football players "hundreds of thousands of dollars" to play for them.

There is one more football scandal that needs mentioning in this chapter. The scandal took place at the high school level, and interestingly enough, the story is about a high school that did not even exist. It's one of the strangest examples of sinning in the religion of football. Years from now this story will be known as — The Bishop Sycamore High School Scandal.

The Bishop Sycamore Centurions were an American football team based in Columbus, Ohio. They claimed to be the high school football team of Bishop Sycamore High School. However, after a blowout loss to IMG Academy that was televised on ESPN on August 29, 2021, there was increased scrutiny and investigation about the school's existence, along with the identities and credentials of the team's administration. A former executive for the Ohio High School Athletic Association came forward to say that after three years of investigating the school, he was convinced that it was a scam. A report conducted by the Ohio Department of Education that was published in December 2021 confirmed the school to be a fraud.

The Ohio Department of Education's investigation discovered that during the 2020–2021 school year, the Ohio Department of Education listed Bishop Sycamore as a "non-chartered, non-tax supported school" and the school was not listed at all for the 2021–2022 year. The state listed a P.O. Box as its mailing address, and its physical address as being a sports training facility in Columbus, Ohio. In 2020, the school claimed an enrollment of only three students. The investigation found that the school failed to meet educational standards, failed to provide a physical location for classes, and did not employ any teachers!

This chapter about sinners in the religion of football shared some disappointing stories at the high school, college and professional level. Perhaps football players, executives and coaches who lie, cheat or steal, simply have a character flaw that needs to be corrected. In the religion of football, the Football Gods welcome a sincere apology and certainly endorse forgiveness. However, when individuals do very terrible things, including physically harming others and show no remorse, they may be spiritually possessed by — The Demons.

CHAPTER SIXTEEN

The Demons

"It is better to conquer yourself than to win a thousand battles. Then the
victory is yours. It cannot be taken from you, not by angels or
by demons, heaven or hell."
—Buddha

A DEMON IS A SUPERNATURAL BEING, TYPICALLY ASSO-
ciated with evil, prevalent historically in religion, occul-
tism, literature, fiction, mythology, and folklore. In several
world religions, a demon is considered an evil spiritual entity with the power to possess living creatures. In
Christianity, it is believed that Satan, among other names
for "the devil," is a spiritual being who rebelled against
God and leads a spiritual legion composed of demons who
oppose God through various schemes that are designed to
keep men and women out of God's Kingdom of Heaven.

Sadly, the battle between the light and the dark, good
and evil, continues to this day on planet earth and the game
of football is a key battleground. This lurking, demonic,
negative energy can take control of the hearts and minds

of people. In recent years, there are a few examples of demonic behavior in the religion of football. The first example involves — Penn State University.

Jerry Sandusky was an assistant college football coach who worked his entire career for head coach Joe Paterno at Pennsylvania State University from 1969 to 1999. Sandusky was an award-winning coach who even wrote books about coaching. However, Sandusky founded a nonprofit charity serving underprivileged and at-risk children and that may have been when the coach fell to the dark side. In 2011, after an extensive investigation, Sandusky was arrested and charged with more than 50 counts of sexual abuse of young boys over a 15-year period. Many of Sandusky's sexual crimes were committed at the university's football facilities on campus. A few years later, this demonic energy forced its way into Waco, Texas, at — Baylor University.

After a five-year investigation undertaken by the NCAA in 2016, it was concluded that the Baylor Football program had a "campus-wide culture of sexual violence." The lawsuits claimed that 31 players at the Christian university committed 52 acts of rape over a four-year period. Making the situation worse, the investigation discovered that Baylor university officials became aware of claims against some of their football players and yet ignored the allegations. The head football coach, Art Briles, was fired and Baylor University's President, Ken Starr, resigned. Players found guilty were sent to jail. Recent examples of demonic behavior can also be found in the National Football League.

There is actually a website (https://databases.usato-day.com/nfl-arrests/) that tracks all of the criminalities of National Football League players since the year 2000. These are arrests, charges, and citations of NFL players for crimes more serious than common traffic violations. Almost all of the players belonged to an NFL roster at the time of the incident. The data comes from media reports and public records. The database was conceived and created by sports reporter Brent Schrotenboer. Many of these crimes relate to domestic violence or driving while intoxicated, while some of the arrests are for murder!

O.J. Simpson, the former running back for the Buffalo Bills, was accused of killing his ex-wife, Nicole Brown Simpson, and her friend Ronald Goldman. Simpson was acquitted of all charges but later found guilty in a civil trial. In a separate case in 2008, Simpson was found guilty on 12 charges, including armed robbery and kidnapping.

Eric Naposki played for the New England Patriots from 1988 to 1997. The former linebacker was found guilty of first-degree murder in the 1994 shooting death of Southern California millionaire William McLaughlin. Naposki had been romantically linked to McLaughlin's girlfriend, who was a $1 million beneficiary on his life-insurance policy.

Rae Carruth, the former wide receiver for the Carolina Panthers, was found guilty in 2001 of conspiracy to commit murder in the drive-by shooting of his girlfriend, who was eight months pregnant with their child. Cherica Adams died, but the child survived. Carruth served almost 20 years in prison. In 2007, quarterback Michael Vick was in the mainstream news almost every day because of — The Bad News Kennels Dog Fighting Scandal.

The Bad Newz Kennels dog fighting investigation began

in April 2007 with a search of a property in Virginia, owned by Michael Vick, who was at the time quarterback for the Atlanta Falcons, and the later discovery of evidence of a dog fighting ring. Over seventy dogs, mostly pit bull terriers, with some said to be showing signs of injuries, were seized by federal authorities. The case drew widespread publicity to the issues of animal abuse and dog fighting. Vick and three others were convicted and sent to prison. Vick was suspended by the National Football League and lost endorsement deals worth millions of dollars.

In 2013, New England Patriots tight end Aaron Hernandez was arrested and later convicted of murder after playing three seasons in the National Football League. During the offseason, Hernandez was arrested and charged for the murder of Odin Lloyd, a semi-professional player who was dating the sister of Hernandez's fiancée. Following his arrest, Hernandez was immediately released by the Patriots. He was found guilty of first-degree murder in 2015 and sentenced to life in prison without the possibility of parole. While on trial for Lloyd's murder, Hernandez was also indicted for the 2012 double homicide of Daniel de Abreu and Safiro Furtado; he was acquitted after a 2017 trial. Days after being acquitted of the double homicide, Hernandez was found dead in his cell, which was ruled a suicide.

During the 2021 NFL season, Las Vegas Raiders wide receiver Henry Ruggs III was driving 156 mph with a blood alcohol level twice the Nevada legal limit. He lost control of the car and crashed into the rear of another vehicle which then burst into flames, killing Tina Tintor, a 23-year-old woman. Also, in 2021, former NFL player Phillip Adams, who played for the Oakland Raiders, committed a mass shooting when he shot and murdered a prominent doctor, his wife, and their two grandchildren before later killing himself. Dr. Robert Lesslie, 70, and his wife, Barbara, 69, were pronounced dead in their home along with grandchildren Adah Lesslie, 9, and Noah Lesslie, 5.

Recognizing that some acts of violence against others are so severe that they are perhaps unforgiveable, the best way for an individual to reduce bad karma and begin building up good karma is to begin a spiritual path towards enlightenment. As readers know from a previous chapter in this book, charity work and community service are very effective ways to make progress on a spiritual journey. During a spiritual transformation, there is usually a purification process of the body, mind, and soul of the seeker. Regarding the body purification process, perhaps the best way for football players to build up good juju, while also building up muscle strength at the same time, is by going — Vegan.

CHAPTER SEVENTEEN

The Vegans

"Vegan. Vegan Strong."
—Cam Newton

VEGANISM IS THE PRACTICE OF ABSTAINING FROM THE use of animal products, particularly in diet. An individual who follows the diet or philosophy is known as a vegan. Dietary vegans refrain from consuming meat, eggs, dairy products, and any other animal-derived substances. An ethical vegan is someone who not only follows a plant-based diet but extends the philosophy into other areas of their lives, opposes the use of animals for any purpose, and tries to avoid any cruelty and exploitation of all animals.

You might be surprised to learn that several of the world's best athletes have gone vegan. For example, some of Ultimate Fighting Championship's most well-known fighters have done so. In Kenny Herzog's article "Why UFC's Toughest Fighters Are Going Vegan," he describes UFC commentator Joe Rogan's post-fight interview with Nate Diaz. Diaz had just defeated UFC Featherweight

Champion Conor McGregor, one of the toughest guys in the world, in a bruising battle. During the interview after the fight, Diaz, who strictly abstains from eating meat, poultry, and dairy, boasts "Who's the real caveman here? Who's the real beast? If anything, meat's gonna slow you down." Veganism is gaining popularity in another tough guy sport too — Football.

At the end of the 2017 season, the Kansas City Chiefs suffered another heartbreaking playoff loss. This time, the Chiefs lost at home to the Tennessee Titans. The Chiefs, who had built up an early 21–3 lead, started losing steam in the fourth quarter while the Titans continued to fight on with increasing vigor. The Titans rallied to win the game 22–21, earning their first playoff win in 14 years. It turns out that almost a dozen members of the Titans were vegans. Most of them played on the defense, so let's take a closer look.

In 2017, the Titans defense ranked third in the National Football League against the run and fifth in the league with a total of 40 quarterback sacks. The Titans' team leader in sacks with five was Wesley Woodyard, a vegan. Regarding his vegan diet, Woodyard told Luke Darby in his 2015 GQ article "The Real-Life Diet of a Vegan NFL Defensive Lineman," "My energy level's gone up...And it's just putting in good fuel to your body. And of course, it's always hard to keep weight on this time of the season. But it's worth it for me staying on top of my health."

Another popular football player, recently retired Chicago Bears defensive lineman David Carter, switched to a 100% plant-based diet in 2014. A typical vegan-day menu for Carter might include oatmeal with hemp protein, bananas and berries for breakfast, brown rice and black beans topped with avocado and cashew cheese for lunch, couscous with onion and garlic, and spinach salad with bell peppers for dinner. According to his interview with *GQ* magazine, Carter tries to eat 1.2 pounds of protein per day in the offseason. He eats 10,000 calories in a normal day, which includes five meals and a number of snacks.

Some nutritionists believe that veganism, in addition to increasing stamina and energy on the playing field, may also lead to career longevity. At 44 years old, Tampa Bay Buccaneers quarterback Tom Brady played again in the Super Bowl to end the 2021 NFL season. What is the secret to his success? According to Dan Pompei of *Bleacher Report*, Brady embraces a unique "body work" approach to fitness that focuses more on the use of rubber resistance bands for high-intensity workouts rather than on power and strength workouts. However, perhaps the real secret to Brady's success and long career is something else. Maybe it's the fact that he carefully adheres to a vegan diet most of the year. Several other prominent National Football League players have joined the vegan movement.

Former Carolina Panthers quarterback Cam Newton has become outspoken about his veganism. Newton was even featured in an advertising campaign in 2020 with PETA (People for the Ethical Treatment of Animals) called "Built Like a Vegan." The movement is spreading to the college ranks too. Recently drafted Chicago Bears quarterback Justin Fields is a vegan and apparently some of his teammates on top ranked Ohio State University's football team were also vegan.

Not only is eating a vegan diet good for a person's health and may improve athletic performance, but a vegan lifestyle also creates good karma. Followers of Hinduism believe that what we eat, or take in, has spiritual energy. The animals people eat have energy. So, if an animal was treated cruelly or died in fear, or in terror, people take that "negative energy" into their bodies. Perhaps this is why some NFL players such as Cam Newton have become so passionate about veganism and have become vegan activists. It's not just about better athletic performance, it's about creating awareness about animal cruelty and spiritual energy.

Former NFL quarterback Colin Kaepernick has become a vegan activist and during the COVID-19 pandemic, his organization called "Know Your Rights" teamed up with Impossible Foods and provided one million free plant-based burgers to those in need. Kaepernick even collaborated with Ben & Jerry's Ice Cream to launch an exclusive vegan ice cream flavor called "Changed the Whirled." Kaepernick's vegan activism is commendable, but his legacy of activism will forever be remembered in the religion of football for speaking out against police brutality. Single-handedly, Colin Kaepernick ignited a social justice movement and for that his story deserves its own chapter called — The Martyr.

CHAPTER EIGHTEEN

The Martyr

"I am not going to stand up to show pride in a flag for a country that oppresses black people and people of color."
—Colin Kaepernick

ACCORDING TO WIKIPEDIA, A MARTYR IS SOMEONE that suffers persecution for advocating, renouncing, or refusing to renounce or advocate, a religious belief or cause as demanded by an external party. In the martyrdom narrative of the remembering community, this refusal to comply with the presented demands results in the punishment or execution of an individual by an alleged oppressor. Originally applied only to those who suffered for their religious beliefs, the term has also come to be used in connection with people mistreated for a political cause. Most martyrs are considered holy or are respected by their followers, becoming symbols of exceptional leadership and heroism in the face of difficult circumstances. Martyrs play significant roles in world religions and secular life. The religion of football has its own martyr — Colin Kaepernick.

In 2016, during the playing of the national anthem at a National Football League game, rather than standing tall and saluting the American flag, a tradition held dearly by patriotic Americans and avid football fans, Colin Kaepernick chose to make a political statement by kneeling down to protest a rash of police brutality incidents in black communities across the country. The NFL team owners, and later even President Trump, felt that Kaepernick's protest was unpatriotic and disrespectful to U.S. soldiers and veterans who have fought and died for their country. Kaepernick, who had very strong feelings on the issue, ignored his critics and continued to kneel during the national anthem at each game for the rest of the season.

To complicate matters, other National Football League players began to follow Kaepernick's lead. Before the NFL team owners knew it, players on almost every team were kneeling during the national anthem. When Kaepernick's contract with the San Francisco 49ers expired, he was not re-signed. More curiously, as a free agent, he could not land another job in the NFL despite being in the prime of his career. As months went by, reporters and fans began to suspect that Kaepernick had been "blackballed."

This conspiracy theory was supported in Jack Moore's article in the *Guardian*, "A Form of Punishment: Colin Kaepernick and the History of Blackballing in Sports." Moore describes a 2017 NFL free-agent market with Kaepernick still without an offer while several less talented players received lucrative deals, including unproven Mike Glennon, career backup Josh McCown, and journeymen Brian Hoyer, Landry Jones, and Matt Barkley. Also, a general manager anonymously told Mike Freeman of the *Bleacher Report* that roughly 70% of NFL teams were unwilling to sign Kaepernick, not because they didn't believe he could play, but as punishment for expressing his political beliefs. One team, the Seattle Seahawks, was willing to sign Kaepernick to a contract but insisted that he agree to stand for the national anthem during every game. When he refused, the Seahawks decided not to sign him and withdrew the offer. Colin Kaepernick never played a snap in the NFL ever again. In the religion of football, Colin Kaepernick had officially become a martyr. With his football playing days behind him, Kaepernick has become an iconic social influencer and philanthropist.

Colin Kaepernick's "Know Your Rights Camp" aims to "advance the liberation and well-being of black and brown communities through education, self-empowerment, mass-mobilization and the creation of new systems that elevate the next generation of change leaders." Kaepernick also founded "The Know Your Rights Camp Legal Defense Initiative" after the George Floyd protests, providing legal resources to activists and protestors. Kaepernick additionally joined the board of *Medium* and writes stories focused on race and civil rights in America. For his charitable giving work, Kaepernick founded the "Colin Kaepernick Foundation," a nonprofit organization with the primary focus of fighting oppression through education and social activism. Kaepernick does the little things too, such as donating his suits to Kevin Livingston's charity called "100 Suits for 100 Men" which provides business attire for job seekers who have recently been released from jail or are suffering economic hardship. Kaepernick's efforts have not gone unnoticed. In 2017, he was awarded the Sports Illustrated Muhammad Ali Legacy Award.

Proving the Football Gods have a sense of humor for poetic justice, even though it's been almost five years since Colin Kaepernick has played in the National Football League, *Madden NFL 22* still has him in the video game as a free agent. The former San Francisco 49ers quarterback received an "81 Rating" which was better than more than half of the starting quarterbacks in the league. Colin Kaepernick, keep doing what you are doing and may the Football Gods always be with you!

CHAPTER NINETEEN

The American Dream

"I have a dream."
—Martin Luther King, Jr.

THE "AMERICAN DREAM" HAS DIFFERENT MEANINGS to different people. Conceptually, its meaning has changed over the years. To Native Americans, even before America got its name, it was the dream of herds of healthy buffalo roaming the plains to provide food throughout the year and clothing to sustain tribes through harsh winters. To the Puritans, the dream was freedom of religion separate from the Church of England and the escape from persecution and possible imprisonment at home. To our forefathers, the dream was rooted in the Declaration of Independence, which proclaims that "all men are created equal" with the same "right to life, liberty and the pursuit of happiness." During the periods of the Industrial Revolution and the California Gold Rush, America became the land of opportunity for a better life with the dream of prosperity, success, and upward mobility through hard work, discovery, and determination. And before and after World Wars I and II, it was the dream of tired, poor, huddled masses of European immigrants sailing into New York Harbor, being welcomed to a new land by the Statue of Liberty.

In more recent times, the concept of the American Dream has found its way into politics. Martin Luther King, Jr. had a dream of an America without racism where every individual had the same civil and economic rights. In its own way, and in this context, football has also played an important role in advancing — The American Dream.

In 2015, Jennifer Welter became the first female coach in the National Football League. Welter served as an intern for the Arizona Cardinals defensive coaching staff. Also, in 2015, Sarah Thomas became the first full-time female NFL official as a referee. In 2021, Thomas became the first woman to officiate in a Super Bowl. With regard to Super Bowls, Jennifer King, an assistant running back coach for the Tampa Bay Buccaneers, became both the first black female assistant coach in the NFL and the first female coach to win a Super Bowl. Women are still a minority in the NFL, but progress is being made. In fact, there are now twelve women coaches and three female referees in the league. Progress is also being made with regard to other minorities finding representation in the NFL.

In February of 2021, the New York Jets announced the hiring of San Francisco 49ers defensive coordinator Robert Saleh as their new head coach. As a result of that hiring, Saleh became the first Muslim to become a head coach of an NFL team. According to a February 11, 2021, article written by the Religion News Service and published in the *Desert News*:

> Saleh's rise to become the first NFL coach of Muslim heritage includes a 10-year career in coaching roles with various NFL and college football teams. Saleh was most recently the defensive coordinator for the San Francisco 49ers, who won the NFC Championship in 2020 before losing to the Kansas City Chiefs in Super Bowl LIV. In Saleh's hometown of Dearborn, Michigan, the Islamic faith and American football have a unique synergy. The town is often described as the largest Arab community outside of the Middle East, many of whom moved to the area in the early 20th century. The school is also noteworthy for being a public school with a majority-Muslim population. A 2011 NPR report noted that 90% of the school's population was Muslim. The cafeteria serves halal food to accommodate its students' religious needs. During the period in which Saleh attended the school, Lebanese Americans made up a plurality of the Arab student population. In his freshman year, the school won its fourth state football championship.

The United States of America is a great melting pot of people from many countries on planet Earth. Almost, if not all, races, religions, and skin colors are represented. The Football Gods certainly look forward to the day when every person has the same opportunity for prosperity, success, and upward mobility for themselves and their children, achieved through good, honest, hard work, in a society that is tolerant and respectful of our individual and religious differences. Only then will the promise of the American Dream truly be fulfilled.

CHAPTER TWENTY

The Golden Age

"This world needs a little more love, compassion, and empathy."
—Julian Edelman

THE TERM "GOLDEN AGE" COMES FROM GREEK mythology. The age depicts a time in human civilization where there is peace, harmony, stability, and prosperity all across the planet. These ages come and go and they can last for hundreds of years. The concept is that humanity lives though epochs of time that are cyclical in nature. Golden Ages do not last forever, and bad times, also known as "Dark Ages," follow if the people lose their moral compass and sever their divine connection with God.

In March of 2021, Duxbury High School, in Massachusetts, fired its successful football coach after an investigation proved that the team used anti-Jewish, also known as anti-Semitic language, including a mention of "Auschwitz," the largest German Nazi death camp where more than a million Jewish people were murdered, in its on-field play calling during a game against Plymouth North

High School. The words "Rabbi" and "Dreidel" were also used. The former head coach released a statement and apologized for his actions. Sadly, this incident was not the only anti-Semitic occurrence at the high school football level in 2021.

In June of 2021, the story broke about football coaches at McKinley High School, in Canton City, Ohio, who made a Jewish football player eat an entire pizza that had pepperoni residue on it as a punishment for skipping a voluntary team workout. The player was told by the coaching staff that if he didn't eat it, he would lose his position on the team. The entire ordeal in the high school gym was caught on video. The teen was shouted at by coaches and teammates as he ate the pizza after removing the slices of pepperoni. The head coach and his seven assistant coaches were fired. Sadly, anti-Semitism also still lingers at the professional football level.

In the summer of 2020, during the NFL offseason, former Philadelphia Eagles wide receiver DeSean Jackson apologized for a series of anti-Semitic Instagram posts over a weekend. In his apology, Jackson claimed that his posts had been misinterpreted. His posts referenced a Jewish plan to "extort America" and achieve "world domination." In his apology, he said that he regretted posting about Hitler, the dictator of Nazi Germany during the genocide of European Jews during World War Two. In a statement he made on Instagram, Jackson said, "Hitler has caused terrible pain to Jewish people like the pain African-Americans have suffered. We should be together fighting anti-Semitism and racism. This was a mistake to post this and I truly apologize for posting it and sorry for any hurt I have caused." Julian Edelman, Super Bowl winning wide receiver with the New England Patriots, who is Jewish, posted his own video on social media to address the DeSean Jackson situation. Edelman had this to say:

> There's no room for anti-Semitism in this world. Even though we're talking about anti-Semitism, I don't want to distract from how important the Black Lives Matter movement is and how we need to stay behind it. I think the Black and Jewish communities have a lot of similarities. One unfortunate similarity is that they are both attacked by the ignorant and the hateful. It's really hard to see the challenges a community can face when you're not part of it, so what we need to do is: We need to listen, we need to learn, we need to act. We need to have those uncomfortable conversations, if we're gonna have real change. So, to that end, DeSean, let's do a deal: How about we go to D.C. and I take you to the Holocaust Museum, and then you take me to the Museum of African-American History and Culture. Afterward, we grab some burgers and we have those uncomfortable conversations. This world needs a little more love, compassion and empathy.

President Ronald Reagan, the 40th U.S. President, said it best during a speech before the United Nations in 1987 in his attempt to unite the countries of world. He said, "Perhaps we need some outside universal threat to make us recognize this common bond. I occasionally think how quickly our differences worldwide would vanish if we were facing an alien threat from outside this world." President Reagan made a compelling point. Humanity, with all of its different races and religions on planet Earth, would quickly unite as one if faced with a potential global threat.

CHAPTER TWENTY

The UFOs

"The aliens came to watch us play."
—Steve Casey

IT IS NO SURPRISE THAT RESEARCH SCIENTISTS HAVE had a longstanding interest in astronomy and the unknown world of outer space. The U.S. military at the Pentagon, NASA (the National Aeronautics and Space Administration), and the airline industry also have a keen interest in what goes on in the air and above the clouds. You may, however, be surprised to learn that the Vatican shares this interest. In the 1500s, the Vatican built the Gregorian Tower to explore the sky and its stars and the Catholic Church is still searching the cosmos today. The Vatican operates its Advanced Technology Telescope at Mount Graham International Observatory, one of the oldest observatories in the world. This giant telescope is not positioned in Vatican City or even in Italy. It's in Arizona.

New Mexico, its neighbor to the east, has had more than its share of conspiracy tales relating to outer space and possible government cover-ups. One of the most famous of these events is the "Roswell Incident," which occurred in New Mexico in mid-1947 when a "flying disc" crashed at a ranch near the town. The U.S. military claimed that it was just an ordinary weather balloon accident, while others came to believe it was an alien spacecraft whose extraterrestrial occupants were captured and detained for research purposes. Even today, it is uncertain whether the flying disc was a balloon or an unidentified flying object (UFO). This is the case notwithstanding that ample evidence exists to suggest that Earth has indeed been visited by extraterrestrials. Believe it or not, there have been several claims of UFO sightings at football games.

In November of 2011, Horizon High School was facing off against Notre Dame Prep in Scottsdale, Arizona. There were many witnesses and a video was posted on YouTube of the encounter and other videos later emerged to corroborate the evidence. At least four bright lights can be seen in the sky over the football field. According to eyewitnesses, the lights would disappear and then reappear and hover motionless, then dance back and forth in a wave motion. Even Horizon High School's head coach, Steve Casey, noticed the lights during the game and joked to his assistant coaches, "The aliens came to watch us play." And get this, in 2011, UFOs also visited — The University of Notre Dame.

On September 3, 2011, the Notre Dame Fighting Irish hosted the University of South Florida Bulls. The game had to be delayed due to a lightning storm. While the game was in delay, many football fans witnessed several unidentified flying objects moving around in the stormy weather. Fans with their iPhones captured videos of the bright orb-like objects as well as a tube-shaped elongated UFO that was hovering around and above Notre Dame Stadium. Witnesses claimed the orbs would fly straight and then make sharp curves, disappearing into the storm clouds. Mysteriously, there have been other UFO sightings at college football stadiums.

In 2014, several football fans witnessed UFOs during a football game between Washington State University and the University of Oregon. Reports were sent to the National UFO Reporting Center. After the game, football fans gathered around together in the parking lot to watch the bright circles of light that danced in the night sky. Witnesses claimed the lights in the sky would blink sporadically and also flashed different colors. Other witnesses claimed that the UFOs hovered for a few seconds before flying away. Yes indeed, there have been UFO sightings at the high school level, at the college level, and even in the National Football League.

He would wait several years after the unforgettable night to talk about it, but in 2016, Green Bay Packers quarterback Aaron Rodgers said in a podcast interview that back in February of 2005, when he was still just an NFL prospect, he was in New Jersey with California Bears football teammate Steve Levy. They heard a siren in the distance while eating dinner, so Rodgers, Levy, and Levy's brother went into the backyard and looked up at the sky. According to Rodgers, there was a large orange object moving across the night sky. As it moved out of sight, Rodgers and Levy looked at each other in awe. A few years went by, but another NFL quarterback had a UFO sighting of his own.

On March 4, 2021, Cleveland Browns quarterback Baker Mayfield was driving in his car near the Lake Travis area in central Texas. The former number one overall draft pick tweeted to his thousands of followers, "Almost 100%, Em and I just saw a UFO drop straight out of the sky on our way home from dinner...we stopped and looked at each other and asked if either of us saw it...Very bright ball of light going straight down out of the sky towards Lake Travis. Anybody else witness this?"

Perhaps seeing a UFO in person is good luck because since Aaron Rodgers had his UFO encounter as a soon to be NFL rookie, he went on to become one the best NFL quarterbacks of all time. And third year quarterback Baker Mayfield led his Cleveland football team to a 2021 playoff game win for the first time since the 1994 season, perhaps breaking a long-standing playoff curse for the Browns.

Interestingly, President Reagan's speech at the U.N. all those years ago may have been spot on. When UFOs and extraterrestrials visit Earth and hover over our football stadiums, could they possibly know which fans in the crowd are Christian, Jewish, Muslim, Hindu, Sikh, or Buddhist? Do you think they would pay attention to the various shades of color of our skin? Think they would notice our sexual preferences? Even if they could notice, would they even care? When humans unite together with love and respect for each other, only then will the promise of the next Golden Age truly be fulfilled.

EPILOGUE

"D.T. was a better person than he was a player, and he was a
Hall of Fame player."

—Peyton Manning

FOOTBALL PLAYER DEMARYIUS THOMAS WAS BORN ON
Christmas Day in Montrose, Georgia, in 1987. His birth
was a blessing, but his childhood may have felt cursed. As
a little boy, police raided his home and arrested his mother
and grandmother for crack cocaine distribution. After his
mother and grandmother were sent to prison, Thomas
was raised by his aunt and uncle. Despite his challenging
upbringing, Thomas developed into an incredible athlete.
Although he excelled at track and field and on the basketball
court, Demaryius Thomas was so good at football that he
earned an athletic scholarship at Georgia Tech University.

After a terrific college football career, wide receiver
Demaryius Thomas was drafted by the Denver Broncos
in the first round and played ten seasons in the National
Football League, mostly with the Broncos. Thomas made

five Pro Bowls during his illustrious career and he became a Super Bowl champion. Along the way in 2011, Thomas played a critical role when Tim Tebow steered the Broncos to a miracle end of the season-winning streak that led to an unlikely playoff berth. When Tim Tebow threw the game-winning 80-yard touchdown pass to defeat the highly favored Pittsburgh Steelers, it was Demaryius Thomas who caught that touchdown. It turns out that like Tim Tebow, Demaryius Thomas was an evangelical Christian who frequently made social media posts about his faith and he even had a tattoo of a portrait of Jesus on his left arm bearing the phrase — Jesus Saves.

On July 13, 2015, Thomas' mother was granted forgiveness by then President Barack Obama, who commuted her sentence at midnight on November 11, 2015. Thomas' mother saw her son play football in person for the first time a year later. On August 2, 2016, Obama commuted the sentence of Thomas' grandmother. The release of his mother and grandmother from prison must have been two of the happiest times in his life. However, the story of Demaryius Thomas has a sad ending.

Demaryius Thomas got into a car crash after driving recklessly in 2019. Police found Thomas was driving over 70 mph in a 30-mph zone at the time of the crash and he had two other people in the car with him. The car rolled multiple times when he lost control on a road in the Denver area. Thomas received one year of probation after pleading guilty to a misdemeanor charge of careless driving resulting in injury. He also received 50 hours of community service and was required to pay fines and restitution. Thomas was injured in the car crash and experienced a series of health problems since.

Sadly, on December 9, 2021, Demaryius Thomas was found dead in his shower at his home. Initial reports suggested that Thomas died from lingering health issues that he had since his tragic car accident, but days after it was revealed from the 911 call to police that Thomas died from a seizure and a heart attack. Thomas was going to turn 34 years young in just two more weeks on Christmas Day.

Just three days after his passing, the Denver Broncos had a home game and made plans to pay tribute to Demaryius Thomas. As fate would have it, the Broncos would be hosting the Detroit Lions. Yes indeed, the same Detroit Lions who just a week prior paid tribute to Oxford High School's hero, Tate Myre. On this football Sunday that was filled with intense emotion, Empower Field at Mile High Stadium held a moment of silence for Thomas and also showed a video tribute just before kickoff. The Broncos players wore #88 stickers on their helmets. Many of the home fans wore Thomas' #88 jerseys and when the Broncos took the field for the first play of the game, they only lined up ten players on purpose to pay tribute to Thomas. The ten Broncos players stood motionless in their formation and let the play clock wind down to zero, giving Thomas another moment of silence. The Detroit Lions responded with a classy move and declined the penalty.

During the game, Football Gods moments were sure to follow. In the fourth quarter, Broncos safety Justin Simmons intercepted Lions quarterback Jared Goff and immediately placed the football between the 8s on the No. 88 painted on the Broncos' sideline at the 10-yard line. The players on the field had honored Thomas once again, but it was time for the Football Gods to pay their respects to #88 as well, and they did it in a way that only the Football Gods know how.

The Denver Broncos defeated the Detroit Lions that day and on the final 14-play touchdown drive, the Broncos traversed, you guessed it — 88 yards. After the game in the locker room, the Broncos players were amazed by the numerology left behind by the Football Gods. Broncos wide receiver Courtland Sutton said to reporters regarding the 88-yard final drive of the game, "That's crazy!" Speaking about the synchronicity, Broncos wide receiver Tim Patrick said, "He's always going to be there for us. I think he's going to be there more in life...yeah, he probably was out there with us." Demaryius Thomas, may your soul rest in peace.

THE AFTERWORD

"When angels visit us, we do not hear the rustle of wings, nor feel
the feathery touch of the breast of a dove; but we know their presence
by the love they create in our hearts."
—Mary Baker Eddy

I FEATURED MY FRIEND PAUL GREENWOOD IN
my first book, *The Baseball Gods are Real*, in the chapter entitled "The 1985 World Series." Paul and I first met
at a party shortly after our families moved to Kansas City
at about the same time in 2012. My family moved to the
Kansas City suburb of Leawood for a change of lifestyle.
Paul and his family moved to the suburbs for a much different reason.

Paul and his wife, Sara, and their two children, Dustin
and Gavin, were living in San Francisco when he learned
that his father, Jimmy Greenwood, had become terminally
ill with cancer. Knowing his dad had only a short time left
to live, Paul gave up his dream job running a charter school
so he could move back home to be near his father. Just a
few months after they relocated, Jimmy Greenwood passed
away. Paul turned to yoga to help him grieve the loss of his
dad and overcome his suffering.

One day my wife Reggie was dropping our children Kayla and Nate off at Sunday school when she saw Paul running out the door with his yoga mat in hand. Paul flew by Reggie in a hurry and said, "Can't talk, late for yoga!" The next week, Reggie told Paul that I also went to yoga class on Sunday mornings. It turns out that Paul and I both participated in Sunday morning yoga classes at the same exact time but at different studios. The next time I saw Paul, we talked about our yoga situation and agreed to start attending classes together every Sunday morning.

Paul and I became very close friends in the months that followed. Paul and I got together for several Kansas City Chiefs football games at Arrowhead Stadium and attended baseball games across the way at Kauffman Stadium to watch our beloved Kansas City Royals. Every time we were at the K, Paul would reminisce and tell stories about how much his dad loved baseball.

One of the baseball stories Paul told me was simply unbelievable. It occurred at the end of Game 7 of the 1985 World Series between the Royals and their cross-state rivals, the St. Louis Cardinals. Paul and his dad were at Kauffman Stadium sitting in the second row behind home plate to the right of the catcher, on the home team side of the field. When the Royals won the game and became World Series champions for the first time ever, the fans went berserk. Some fans, for a brief moment, lost their minds. Paul's dad was one of them. He was so excited that the Royals won the World Series that he hopped over the front row seats and ran onto the field to celebrate with the team and other exuberant fans. The only problem was that he completely forgot about his young son, Paul, and left him alone in his seat.

Paul experienced a unique set of emotions. On the one hand, he was thrilled, like everyone else, that the Royals had just won their first World Series. On the other hand, he was terrified because he had just witnessed his father get tackled to the ground by two police offices, dragged to a chair, and then handcuffed. Paul tried desperately to get the attention of another police officer and one finally came over. Paul explained to the cop that the guy handcuffed to the chair on the field was his dad. The police officer picked Paul up, carried him across the field, and sat him down on his dad's lap.

Together, Paul and his dad watched the Royals and their fans celebrate from the best seat in the house. After a few minutes, the police officer that had handcuffed Jimmy Greenwood came over and said, "Aw, screw it." The cop took out his keys, unlocked the handcuffs, and set Jimmy free. The Greenwood boys ran away from that chair like two convicts escaping from Alcatraz, but instead of heading to the exits, Paul and his dad ran around the bases at Kauffman Stadium and touched them all.

Surprisingly, Game 7 of that 1985 World Series has taken on another special meaning for me as well. While writing *The Music Gods are Real, Vol. 2*, I became friends with fellow author and baseball lover, Joe Bonsall, who also happens to be the tenor for the legendary country music quartet — The Oak Ridge Boys. I even travelled to Branson, Missouri, to interview Joe and attended one of the group's very entertaining shows at the famous Mansion

Theater. Who sang the National Anthem before the start of Game 7 at Kauffman Stadium that day? If you guessed The Oak Ridge Boys, you would be correct. You simply can't make this stuff up.

Sadly, just when Paul seemed to have finally overcome the loss of his father, additional grief surfaced. A few years later, Paul's mom, Sharon Greenwood, found out that she too had cancer. Sharon had fought off cancer many years before as a young adult, and now, after difficult sessions of chemotherapy and radiation treatments, it appeared that she was able to fend off cancer once again. Or so we thought. Unfortunately, Sharon's cancer resurfaced with a vengeance. This time, her doctors reported that it had spread throughout her body. After another long battle, during which all experimental therapies failed, Sharon notified her family and friends that she would discontinue further treatment. Just a few weeks later, Sharon Greenwood passed away surrounded by her loved ones. The funeral was set for the morning of February 2, 2020 — Super Bowl Sunday.

Super Bowl Sunday was a winter day in Kansas City that should have been windy and cold, probably with a threat of snow. However, the Football Gods would not let that happen. They made sure that the day of Sharon Greenwood's funeral was spring-like, with sunny skies and, believe it or not, temperature that reached 70 degrees. During the rabbi's eulogy at the funeral service, I learned how much Sharon Greenwood loved her family, classical music, the Kansas City Royals and the Kansas City Chiefs.

During the funeral service, Paul's sister Karen told another Greenwood family story that will also stay with me forever. Sharon and Jimmy had gotten engaged and, with the help of their parents, planned their wedding day. Guest lists were prepared, invitations were printed, and the venue for the affair was booked. After all that was in place, the newlyweds to be discovered that their special day was on the same day that the Super Bowl was scheduled to be played. Since Sharon and Jimmy were both dedicated football fans, they actually rescheduled their wedding day so they could watch and enjoy the Super Bowl together.

After the funeral service, I spent the afternoon with Paul at his home to mourn with him and his family. When it was time for me to leave, I hugged Paul, offered my condolences again, and headed home. I knew that my wife Reggie had invited some of her high school friends over to watch the big game, so I wanted to get back in time to help her prepare for our guests. Just before it was time for the Super Bowl to start, I got a call from my Uncle Eddie, my dad's older brother, who lives in Danville, California, located about 30 miles east of San Francisco.

Uncle Eddie called to wish me and my Chiefs good luck. He also challenged me to a bet on who would win the game. He said we could wager a small amount of money, but he thought it would be more fun to bet something silly, like a pair of underwear. I accepted his silly underwear bet but warned him, as all good trash talking sports fans would do, that there was no chance of me losing this bet. I told him that the Football Gods would be supporting the Kansas City Chiefs, and I told him the reason why — Sharon Greenwood.

The Kansas City Chiefs and the San Francisco 49ers

played an epic football game that day, perhaps one of the best Super Bowl games ever played. With just nine minutes to go in the fourth quarter, down by ten points, 20–10, with third down and long, the Chiefs needed a first down to keep the drive and their chances alive. At that point, I yelled out loud in desperation in front of my family and house guests, "Sharon Greenwood, you can't let Paul lose today!" Quarterback Patrick Mahomes took the next snap and immediately threw a towering pass in the direction of Tyreek Hill who made an unbelievable jumping catch for the first down. That play was the turning point. Momentum switched and from that point on, it was all Kansas City. The Chiefs went on to score 21 unanswered points, won the game by a score of 31–20, and accomplished one of the greatest comebacks in Super Bowl history.

Maybe it was a coincidence, maybe not. Maybe it was a wink from the universe. Who knows? But on the sad day that Sharon Greenwood was buried, her favorite football team, the Kansas City Chiefs, won the Super Bowl for the first time in 50 years. As time ran out on the clock and the game ended, I vividly recall looking at Reggie, Kayla and Nate and said, "The Football Gods are Real."

THE ACKNOWLEDGEMENTS

Reggie, Kayla and Nate Fink, The Blue Valley North Mustangs

Beth and Jeffrey Fink, The New York Jets & Giants fans

Sam Devinki, The Kansas City Chiefs fan

Eddie Fink, The San Francisco 49ers fan

Tate Myre, The Hero

Demaryius Thomas, The #88

Paul, Sara, Gavin, Dustin, Karen, Sharon and Jimmy Greenwood, The 2019 Super Bowl

Rabbi Moshe Grussgott, The Philadelphia Eagles fan

Tim Tebow, The Saint

Colin Kaepernick, The Martyr

Charles "Bad Luck Chuck" Penn, The Curse of the Kansas City Chiefs

Willie Fritz, The Good Karma of the Tulane Green Wave

The Kansas City Chiefs, The Missionaries

Nate Diaz, Tom Brady, Colin Kaepernick, Wesley Woodyard,
Cam Newton, David Carter and Justin Fields, The Vegans

Jennifer Welter, Jennifer King and Robert Saleh,
The American Dream

DeSean Jackson and Julian Edelman, The Golden Age

Damon Wells and the Jefferson High School Football Team,
The Superstitions

Jay Civetti and the Tufts University Football Team, The Rituals

Aaron Rodgers, Steve Levy, Baker Mayfield, The UFO's

Brent Schrotenboer, Ryan McGee, Chris Blake, Josh Peter,
Kenny Herzog, Ron Dicker, Luke Darby, Jack Moore, Mike
Freeman, Leigh Oleszezak, Sydney Van Gorp, Sam Weitzman,
Brandon Alisoglu, Aiken Drum, The Religious News Service,
The Sportswriters

Vicky Millard, The Medium

Brian Smith, Louie Brewer, Gary McKenzie, Anthony Stratton,
The Zealots

Ricky Ciccone, Robert Saleh, Steve Casey, Ron Rivera, Sean
Payton, Greg Williams, Bill Belichick, Marty Schotteneheimer,
Ted Cox, Buddy Teevens, Tommy Bowden, Tommy O'Boyle,
Chris Scelfo, Hank Stram, Andy Reid, Knute Rockne, Jimbo
Fisher, Tom Herman, Jack Del Rio, Damon Wells, Jay Civetti,
Jim Harbaugh, Dan Campbell, Dan Mullen, Hugh Freeze, Dabo
Sweeney, Tom Landry, Tony Dungy, Joe Gibbs, Dan Reeves,
The Football Coaches

Terrell Owens, Brian Hoyer, Landry Jones, Matt Barkley, Mike
Glennon, Tim Patrick, Courtland Sutton, Justin Simmons, Tom
Brady, Sorrell Brown, Shaun King, Anthony Sherman, Derrick

Nnadi, Tyrann Matthieu, Tyreek Hill, Eddie George, Daunte Culpepper, Donovan McNabb, Shaun Alexander, Vince Young, Brett Farve, Larry Fitzgerald, Troy Polamalu, Drew Brees, Peyton Hillis, Adrian Peterson, Oden Beckham, Jr., Ray Lewis, Rob Gronkowski, Travis Kelce, Juju Smith-Schuster, Patrick Mahomes, Jack Chevigny, George Gipp, Myles Brennan, Anthony Richardson, Jalen Wydermyer, Chris Hanson, Jordan Whittington, Carson Wentz, Nick Foles, DeAndre Hopkins, Marshawn Lynch, Payton Manning, Phillip Rivers, Mike Williams, Aiden Hutchinson, Kirk Cousins, Jalen Elliot, Jared Goff, Amon-Ra St. Brown, Curtis Martin, Hayden Wells, Brody Smith, Zack Thomas, Winton Blount, Jay Taylor, Dan Dewing, J.P. Garcia, Matthew Alswanger, Greg Holt, Michael Urlacher, Luke Kuechly, Chris Thompson, Matt Bryant, Michael Dickson, Devante Adams, The Football Players

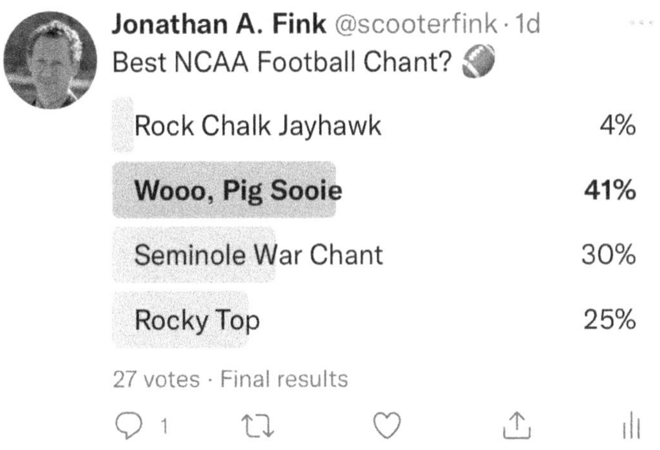
Jonathan A. Fink @scooterfink · 1d
Best NCAA Football Chant? 🏈
Rock Chalk Jayhawk 4%
Wooo, Pig Sooie 41%
Seminole War Chant 30%
Rocky Top 25%
27 votes · Final results
1

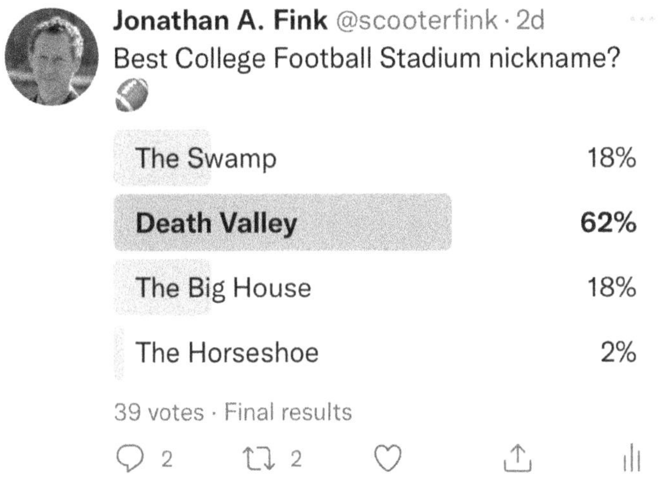
Jonathan A. Fink @scooterfink · 2d
Best College Football Stadium nickname? 🏈
The Swamp 18%
Death Valley 62%
The Big House 18%
The Horseshoe 2%
39 votes · Final results
2
2

Jonathan A. Fink @scooterfink · 4d   ...
Most influential person in the NFL today is?

Tom Brady	**59%**
Aaron Rodgers	15%
Colin Kaepernick	9%
Roger Goodell	17%

34 votes · Final results

♡   ↻   ♡   ↑   ili

Jonathan A. Fink @scooterf... · 12/12/21 ...
Writing a chapter about football rivalries.
Best NFL rivalry is? 🏈 📚

Packers v. Bears	**50%**
Raiders v. Chiefs	13%
Giants v. Eagles	13%
Ravens v. Steelers	24%

24 votes · Final results

♡ 2   ↻ 1   ♡   ↑   ili

Jonathan A. Fink @scooterf... · 12/10/21 ···
Researching for a chapter called The
Traditions. NCAA Football program with the
best traditions?

Wisconsin	11%
Notre Dame	**52%**
Texas A & M	19%
Iowa	18%

27 votes · Final results

Jonathan A. Fink @scooterfink · 5d
Best NCAA Football mascot? 🏈

Sparty - Michigan State	5%
The Tree - Stanford	20%
Donald Duck - Oregon	**55%**
Leprechaun - Notre Dame	20%

20 votes · Final results

💬   🔁   ♡   ⬆   ᶦᶫᶦ

Jonathan A. Fink @scooterfink · 12/8/21 ···
Writing a chapter called The Tailgate. Best
NFL Tailgate is held by? 🏈 📚

Buffalo Bills fans	**56%**
Kansas City Chiefs fans	19%
New York Giants fans	19%
Las Vegas Raiders fans	6%

16 votes · Final results

💬　　🔁　　♡ 1　　⬆️　　ᵢᵢᵢ

Jonathan A. Fink @scooterf... · 12/14/21 ···
Writing a chapter for The Football Gods are
Real called The Sinners? NFL's worst
scandal? 🏈 📚

Patriots - Spygate	10%
Patriots - Deflategate	**50%**
Saints - Bountygate	40%

10 votes · Final results

💬　　🔁　　♡ 3　　⬆️　　ᵢᵢᵢ

Jonathan A. Fink @scooterfink · 12/8/21   ···
Writing a chapter about football rivalries.
Best college football rivalry is? 🏈 📚

Ohio State v. Michigan	**58%**
Auburn v. Alabama	8%
Army v. Navy	17%
Texas v. Oklahoma	17%

36 votes · Final results

💬 2   🔁 1   ♡ 2   ⬆   ᵢₗᵢ

Jonathan A. Fink @scooterfink · 1d   ···
Who will represent the NFC in the Super
Bowl? 🏈

Cowboys	19%
Packers	**54%**
Bucs	19%
Rams	8%

26 votes · Final results

💬   🔁   ♡   ⬆   ᵢₗᵢ

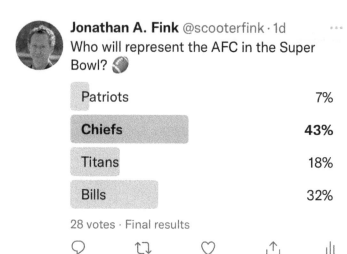

Jonathan A. Fink
@scooterfink

Who will win AFC Championship Game? @NFL @Chiefs @Bengals 🏈

Bengals	45%
Chiefs	**55%**

20 votes · Final results

 **Jonathan A. Fink**
@scooterfink

Who will win NFC Championship
Game? @NFL @RamsNFL @49ers

Rams	**72%**
49ers	28%

18 votes · Final results

 **Jonathan A. Fink**
@scooterfink

Who will win The Super Bowl?

Rams	36%
Bengals	**64%**

58 votes · Final results

JANUARY 12, 2020
The Curse of the Kansas City Chiefs
Divisional Round (Chiefs vs. Texans)

JANUARY 19, 2020
The Curse of the Kansas City Chiefs
AFC Championship (Chiefs vs. Titans)

HALLOWEEN 2019
The Zealots

HALLOWEEN 2021
The Zealots

DECEMBER 12, 2021
The Faithful
Arrowhead Stadium

DECEMBER 12, 2021
The Rivalry Game
Arrowhead Stadium - Chiefs vs. Raiders

The Religion of Football
@FootballGods44 · 8/4/22

Book cover design proces underway🏈

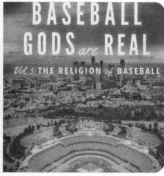

The Religion of Football
@FootballGods44 · 8/4/22

This book is dedicated to Tate Myer, The Hero...🏈

complex.com
Oxford Football Player Reportedly Killed While
Trying to Disarm School Shooter

The Religion of Football
@FootballGods44 · 8/4/22

Chapter about Colin Kaepernick called -The Martyr
@Kaepernick7 ⚡

The Religion of Football
@FootballGods44 · 8/5/22

on3.com
Michigan football standouts, from 'special' to 'gift
from the gods'

The Religion of Football
@FootballGods44 · 8/6/22

The Faithful....🏈

The Religion of Football
@FootballGods44 · 8/6/22

Where it all began....

The Religion of Football
@FootballGods44 · 8/6/22

Chapter called "The Sinners"....🏈

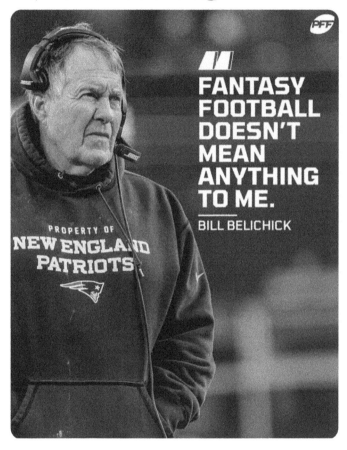

The Religion of Football
@FootballGods44 · 8/6/22

Chapter called "The Cathedrals"

The Religion of Football
@FootballGods44 · 8/6/22

The Vegan.... 🏈

The Religion of Football
@FootballGods44 · 8/7/22

Best football video game of all time...

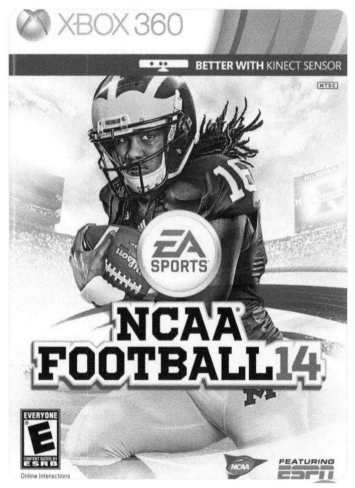

The Religion of Football
@FootballGods44 · 8/11/22

Teams that pray together, win together...🏈

The Religion of Football
@FootballGods44 · 8/16/22

The Saint... 🏈

The Religion of Football
@FootballGods44 · 8/16/22

The Rituals....🏈

The Religion of Football
@FootballGods44 · 8/21/22

Willie Fritz, Tulane's head football coach understands the importance of good team chemistry....

> **Kurt Hester** @TheKurtHester · 8/20/22
>
> Tulane Green Wave only team in the country that 2nd lines though the French Quarter to end fall camp!
> #WaveBrotherhood

Big Game Boomer
@BigGameBoomer · 8/21/22

Traditions like Ralphie's Run are what make College
Football so great. Add this to your bucket list. It's
WILD.

The Religion of Football
@FootballGods44 · 8/23/22

The Cathedrals…. 🏈

 Unnecessary Roughness ✔ @Un… · 8/23/22

A look at the proposed stadium for the Miami Hurricanes.

60,000 seats.

The Religion of Football
@FootballGods44 · 4d

The Fanatics... 🏈

 **Unnecessary Roughness** ✓ @UnnecR... · 5d

Nebraska could play on Mars and their fans
would still show up

The Religion of Football
@FootballGods44 · 3d

The Rituals....🏈

 Unnecessary Roughness ✔ @UnnecR... · 4d

UNLV slot machine >>>>

 Seth Stringer
@SethSnwfdn · 4d

Best HS football student section in the country. 🎉
🏈👀 @Niceville_FB

0:04

The Religion of Football
@FootballGods44 · 4d

The Rituals….

New Orleans Saints ✔ @Saints · 4d

Black and gold tonight ⚜

@CallawayMarquez 🤝 @tayynation1

#Saints | @EAMaddenNFL

Sportskeeda Pro Football ✓ ···
@SKProFootball · 8/24/22

Why is Colin Kaepernick excluded from Madden 23?
NFL continues to blackball ex-49ers QB

sportskeeda.com
Colin Kaepernick excluded from Madden 23 as
NFL continues to blackball ex-49ers QB

The Religion of Football
@FootballGods44 · 8/21/22

The Legend....🏈

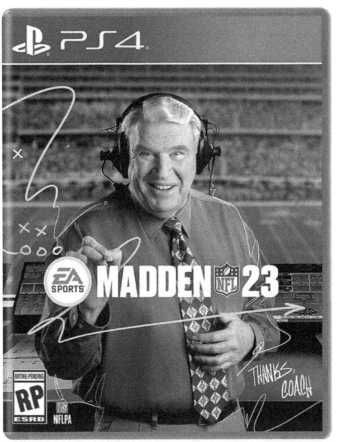

The Religion of Football
@FootballGods44 · 6d

Rest In Peace Len Dawson....

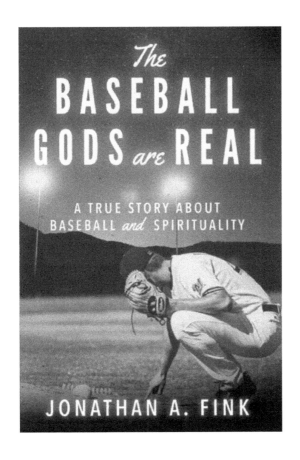

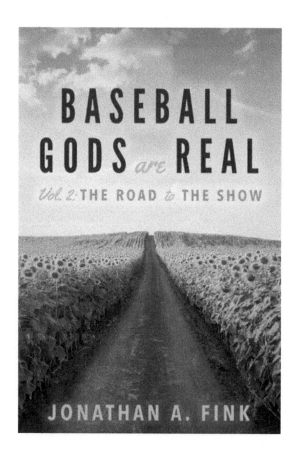

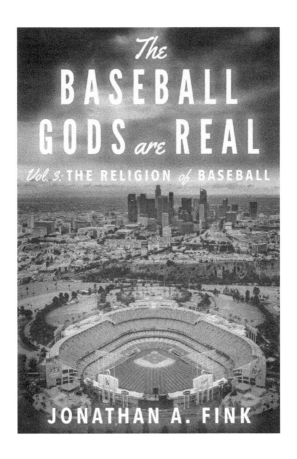

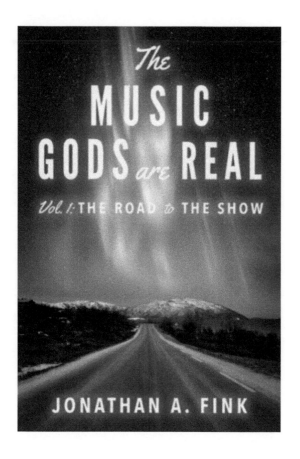